Fikr Taunsvi was the pen name of Ram Lal Bhatia (7 October 1918–12 September 1987), a noted Urdu satirist and columnist, born in Taunsa Sharif, which now lies in Pakistan. He is most well known for his popular column of social satire, 'Pyaz ke Chhilke', or 'Onion Skins', that he wrote for the Urdu daily *Milap*. Fikr published over twenty books in Urdu, including *Chhata Darya, Chaupat Raja, Fikriyat, Fikr Bani, Fikr Nama, Aakhri Kitab*, and at least eight in Hindi. He also wrote social comedy for television, including the series *Fikr ne Kaha* with a writer, Fikr, as its central character.

Maaz Bin Bilal (b. 1986) is associate professor in literary studies at the liberal arts school of Jindal Global University. He earned his PhD from Queen's University Belfast in 2015 for his dissertation on the politics of friendship in E.M. Forster's work. Maaz is also a translator, poet, and critic. He was Charles Wallace Fellow in Writing and Translation in Wales in 2018. *Ghazalnama: Poems from Delhi, Belfast, and Urdu* published in 2019 is his first collection of poems.

Praise for *The Sixth River*

'Written as a journal in Urdu by Fikr Taunsvi, this is a rare and refreshing first person account of the mayhem and death that enveloped Lahore between August and November 1947 as the British Raj came to its convulsive end in Punjab. Deftly combining social satire with political critique, Taunsvi anticipates Saadat Hasan Manto's partition fiction, written after 1948, while displaying a more skeptical view of human frailties in general and politicians in particular than the Urdu story writer. Translated into accessible English, *The Sixth River* is a most welcome addition to the burgeoning personal narratives on Punjab's and India's Partition and will be read widely by students and scholars.'—Ayesha Jalal, Mary Richardson Professor of History, Tufts University

'Direct, despairing, satirical, and heartbreaking, Fikr Taunsvi's first person account of the violent moment of India and Pakistan's birth, is rendered here in a powerful translation. The author's seething anger, his deep confusion about belonging, unbelonging, friendship, love, home, nation and boundaries fill the pages of this journal and bring to the often arid terrain of history a sense of how it is lived on the ground, experienced on the body and felt in the heart.'—Urvashi Butalia, Feminist writer, publisher and author of *The Other Side of Silence: Voices from the Partition of India*

'In Fikr Taunsvi's extraordinary *The Sixth River*, an exquisite translation by Maaz Bin Bilal, Partition has an aural quality, it sounds through questions, rumours, outcry, and the responses that the very fact of Partition silences. This searing text of a psychological and physical journey that propels one man across a border is the story of a collective defeat, of how hate equally tears asunder the lives of those who are misled by it as well as those who could never distinguish between nation states, political leaders, and Hindus and Muslims.'—Ayesha Kidwai, Professor of Linguistics, Jawaharlal Nehru University, and translator of Anis Kidwai's *In Freedom's Shade*

'Fikr Taunsvi's *Chhata Darya*, newly translated as *The Sixth River* by Maaz Bin Bilal, is one of the key memoirs to appear in the wake of the Partition. This atypical ironic record of Fikr's experiences and thoughts in the months leading up to his decision to migrate from Lahore to India some time after the Partition, along with Manto's writings, provides crucial literary testimony to widespread historical trauma in the wake of 1947. Long overdue, this translation of the complete memoir by Maaz Bin Bilal is an important contribution to the evolving discourse on the Partition and its afterlife.'—Tarun K. Saint, author, *Witnessing Partition*

'*Chhata Darya* or *The Sixth River* is a project of historical recovery. From the literary vault, Maaz Bin Bilal translates and brings to us the journals of Fikr Taunsvi, born Ram Lal Bhatia, and known for his satirical writing in Urdu. He belongs to an era which may seem alien in contemporary India and Pakistan, but which epitomised the spirit of the pre-Partition Punjab. Taunsvi wrote his journals in the moments during the passage of Partition, representing and capturing and reflecting some of the raw emotions of that time. His journals are one of the first, direct eye-witness responses, recording and documenting his impressions of the fast-changing landscape around him. The rupture of 1947 radiated far and deep from the terra firma on which it was territorially effected and these critical memoirs—translated here from Urdu—are emblematic of those layers of tragedies, in which not only territory but people and language, region and culture, were also ruptured. At a time when there is a renewed fragmentation, narrowing of critical discourse and attempted homogenising of nation and people, Taunsvi's work deserves a wider audience and Bilal has done a tremendous job.'—Pippa Virdee, Senior Lecturer in Modern South Asian History at De Montfort University, Leicester, and author of *From the Ashes of 1947: Reimagining Punjab*

The
SIXTH RIVER

A Journal from the Partition of India

FIKR TAUNSVI

Translated by MAAZ BIN BILAL

SPEAKING TIGER PUBLISHING PVT. LTD
4381/4, Ansari Road, Daryaganj
New Delhi 110002

Copyright © Phool Kumar Bhatia

Translation, Introduction and
Notes copyright © Maaz Bin Bilal 2019

Published in English by Speaking Tiger in hardback 2019

ISBN: 978-93-89231-17-5
eISBN: 978-93-89231-16-8

10 9 8 7 6 5 4 3 2 1

The moral rights of the author and the translator
have been asserted.

All rights reserved.
No part of this publication may be reproduced, transmitted,
or stored in a retrieval system, in any form or by any means,
electronic, mechanical, photocopying, recording or otherwise,
without the prior permission of the publisher.

This book is sold subject to the condition that it shall not,
by way of trade or otherwise, be lent, resold,
hired out, or otherwise circulated, without
the publisher's prior consent, in any form
of binding or cover other than that
in which it is published.

Contents

Introduction 11

Note on the Translation 31

Author's Note: This Diary 35

Mobbed by Darkness 39

What Place Is This? 87

Come, Let Us Look for the
Dawn Again 133

Appendix I: The Fikr Bibliography 175

Translator's Acknowledgements 177

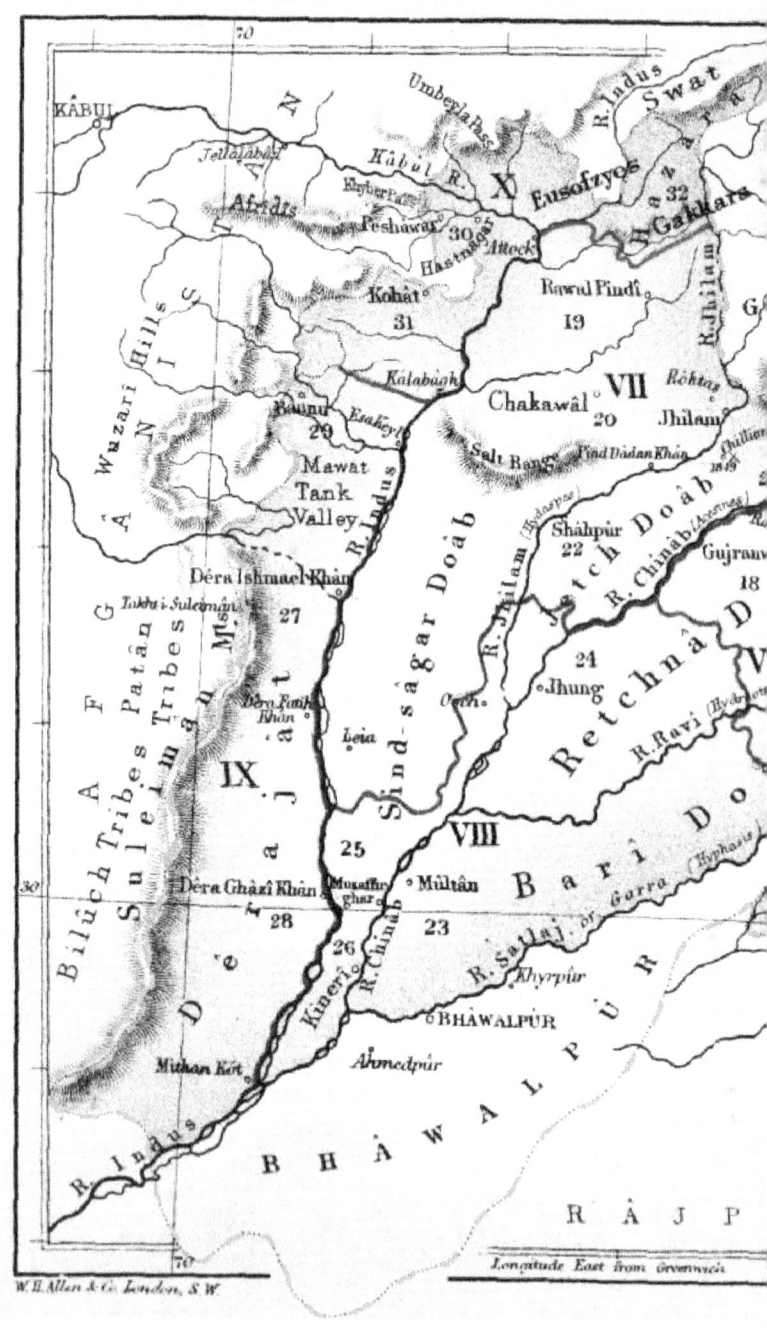

The United Punjab in 1880
Source: Wikimedia Commons

Introduction

The Sixth River is the journal of Fikr Taunsvi, the immensely popular and critically-noted Urdu satirist and columnist, from the time of the Partition of India. It is his eyewitness account of the sundering of the Punjab, while living in Lahore from August to November 1947 until he migrates to Amritsar in post-colonial India, leaving behind his beloved city in the newly created Pakistan. Fikr feels passionately about and reflects deeply upon the tragic political and social events, giving us a journal which becomes a Partition text like no other. Here, a poet and literary writer comments on the trauma of the migration and violence, and the politics that allowed it, through dark satire and irony, but also from personal experience as an eventual migrant and refugee. In *The Sixth River*, Fikr stands out as an inimitable descriptor and thinker for what he describes of Partition-related events, the violence and politics, as well as the lives of other notable intellectuals and artists, and presents it all in his evocatively harrowing, self-deprecating, deeply ironic and reflective prose.

The Fikr of Taunsa Sharif

Fikr Taunsvi (7 October 1918–12 September 1987), born Ram Lal Bhatia, abjured his given name, calling it 'vahyaaat' or 'absurd'* or even 'fake'** and preferred to be known and addressed by his takhallus or pen name. Fikr from Urdu can variously mean: thought, consideration, reflection; deliberation, opinion, notion, idea, imagination, conceit; counsel, advice; care, concern, solicitude, anxiety, grief, sorrow.† Taunsvi implies 'hailing from Taunsa Sharif', a city in the Dera Ghazi Khan Tehsil of western Punjab that now lies in Pakistan. The city is noted for its numerous Sufi shrines. Fikr hailed the shrine of Khwaja Sulaiman Rasul in particular, which was patronized by both Hindus and Muslims.‡ Taken together, the two epithets form a pen name that best describes Fikr's personality, aspirations and concerns. A deep and sensitive thinker, he engaged strongly with and reflected closely upon life and the human condition, as someone who engaged in fikr or may even be considered a fakir in the truest sense of the word. His cultural identity as a Punjabi with his roots in the composite Sufi culture of Taunsa Sharif

---

*In *Warrant Giraftari*, 1966.

**In interview to Dr Muzaffar Hanfi (*Beeswi Sadi*).

†Platts, John Thompson. *A Dictionary of Urdu Classical Hindi and English*. 1881.

‡Op cit. Hanfi.

shaped his pluralistic worldview. His humble origin from a small town and growing up with poor parents also meant (as he recognized himself) that he wrote for them, or the poor.* This is amply reflected in Fikr's work.

Fikr, the thinker, is also self-critical enough to admit that his father was a wily shopkeeper and businessman, who sold to and cheated Baluch tribal customers at the edge of Taunsa Sharif, which he claims lay at the western edge of colonial India. Due to moral indignation against his father's corrupt practices and 'exploitation' of the tribals, and his refusal to provide for his further studies, Fikr left home in 1934 after high school. He wandered across the Punjab, moving through Dera Ghazi Khan, Jampur, Multan, Lyallpur and Sheikhupura, before settling in Lahore, where he found employment eventually with editorial offices of newspapers and started to practice writing seriously.** It was also in Lahore that he found the culture that he had yearned for, but could have never acquired in the peripheral town of Taunsa.

Fikr started off as a poet in Lahore, publishing his first poem in the newspaper *Adabi Duniya* and subsequently his poem 'Tanhai' in the annual anthology published by the Modernist group, Halqa Arbab-e-

---

*Op Cit. *Warrant Giraftari*, 1966.

**Op cit. Hanfi.

Zauq. He also found work first as a clerk then as an editor at *Adab-e-Lateef*, and later at *Savera*, which he edited with his friend, the short-story writer, Mumtaz Mufti. Fikr has described *Savera* as a Progressive or socialist-leaning magazine, while *Adab-e-Lateef* too started off in this manner, but soon turned more Modernist. Thus, Fikr had occasion to absorb the two key strands of art and creative writing dominant in the subcontinent at the time. This also explains his intellectual agility and deep sensitivity to both craft and human issues. Fikr also continued to educate himself by frequenting the Maktaba in Lahore where leading Progressives such as Rajinder Singh Bedi, Ismat Chughtai and Saadat Hasan Manto used to visit.

Fikr's first poetry collection *Hayule* (shadowy forms, apparitions) was published from Lahore too, in 1947, during the tumultuous events of Partition, and he laments the book being left behind in Pakistan. Lahore for him, as one reads in *The Sixth River* too, became the city of (composite) culture and the arts, intellectual inquiry, and creative and professional opportunity. But perhaps even more strongly, Lahore for Fikr was the place of friends, of his genteel society, camaraderie and social etiquette. This love for Lahore and all the values it stood for was the reason the Partition hit him even harder.

The experience of Partition violence as witness and victim, through personal threats and loss, and the undesired migration completed under duress, seem to have shaped his writing career thereon. Fikr largely gave up poetry as a response, and had said in interviews that poetry could not pay the bills, but also that he wished to connect with people in more accessible language. One can also infer from the preferred mode of his subsequent writing—social satire—that Partition shook him out of Romance. Even if it could not shake his sense of social responsibility and commitment, the subsequent writing is filled with gentle humour which is laughing at the world and the self, prodding for moral improvement but not reliant upon it.

Fikr 'Tanzvi'—The Satirist

It is, in fact, his popular column of social satire, 'Pyaz ke Chhilke', or 'Onion Skins'* for the Urdu Daily *Milap* that made Fikr a household name. It was widely held to be the main reason that the newspaper was bought by the bulk of its readership, comprising of students and teachers, doctors and rickshaw-pullers. When I told my senior colleague Prof. Jagdish Batra of Sonipat that I was translating Fikr Taunsvi's work, I got a delighted congratulatory response where he recounted how he learnt the Urdu script only to read

---

*Selected translations by the translator forthcoming from Speaking Tiger in 2020.

Fikr's column, having earlier relished it being read out to him by his father. Such was the impact of Fikr's gentle humour and satire that it prompted his readers and listeners not only to purchase the newspaper but to learn Urdu as well. Can there be any greater effect than that of a writer prodding people to learn the script of a language?

Fikr comes from the long tradition of Urdu tanz-o-mazah or satire and humour. Ali Javad Zaidi, the Urdu literary historian, called him 'a giant among humorists'.* Following on the impact of the *Awadh Punch*, the Urdu satirical weekly published from Lucknow, from 1877 to 1936, and the preeminent Patras Bokhari (1898–1958), it was Fikr who was most 'ingenious in spotting humorous situations, pretending to innocence and unravelling mysteries', commanding a 'vast range' with 'the natural flow in his humour knit[ting] puzzling images of fun and frolick, of sarcasm and exposure, now playing a pleasant companion and now a social reformer.'** It was for this prowess as master of satire or tanz, that a stalwart of Urdu creative prose and author of a number of powerful tales from Partition, Krishan Chander, called Fikr Taunsvi 'Fikr Tanzvi' or Fikr the Satirist, while punning on his pen name and 'satire'.

---

*Zaidi, Ali Javad, *A History of Urdu Literature*. New Delhi: Sahitya Akademi, 1993. 2017. p.426.

**Ibid. p. 427.

In a writing career of over forty years, Fikr wrote over twenty books in Urdu and at least eight in Hindi, apart from the column 'Pyaz ke Chhilke', which he wrote for *Milap* for twenty-five years. Most of these are in the genre of tanz-o-mazah. Some of his notable books are: *Chaupat Raja, Fikr Bani, Professor Budhu, Fikriyat* and *Badnaam Kitab*.*

However, this golden period of Fikr as a writer of genial social satire and easy wit and humour, which began in the 1950s and continued almost till the end of his life, was punctuated or separated from his earlier life as a poet by the tragic Partition of India in 1947, in response to which he wrote the deeply pained, and often darkly ironic works such as *Satwan Asmaan* (The Seventh Sky), *Wagah Canal* and *Chhata Darya* or *The Sixth River*. Thus, the Partition texts, and particularly *The Sixth River*, seem to become the pivot around which Fikr's own career changes course. Having undergone tremendous pain and trauma, the author can neither be a romantic optimist, nor a revolutionary, but only laugh for the rest of his life at the human comedy. But in *The Sixth River*, published within a year of his experiences of Partition, he gives us his autobiographical journal, eyewitness account and political commentary of Partition in a darkly satirical tone with his characteristic bite, which works as a

---

*Complete list given in Appendix I.

uniquely powerful and important text that resonates strongly till date with the Indian subcontinent, which continues to feel the ripples of the long partition.*

Radcliffe's River: Of Blood and Fire

Fikr's sixth river is the metaphorical river for the divisive rift created in the middle of Punjab or the land of five (panj) rivers (āb) by communal and imperial politics, ultimately resulting in what Fikr calls the gigantic snake of Sir Cyril Radcliffe's that was let loose to bisect his beloved Punjab.** Suhail Azimabadi in his preface to *Chhata Darya* interprets the sixth river, thus, to be the Radcliffe line that divides Pakistan and India. On the other hand, Fikr in his own introduction to the journal, describes it as a river of fire and blood that flowed across the Punjab during those times of turmoil. In *The Sixth River*, bombs explode, gunfire sounds through the night, communal rioting goes on unabated, even after azadi; there is murder of innocents, arson, pillaging and occupation of properties, rape and abduction of women, corruption in the forces and camps, desperate attempts at survival, and other failures of humans that continue to fill and fuel this river of blood and fire—all of which Fikr witnesses and records. At one point

---

*See Wazira Zamindar for a theorization of the long partition.

**p. 63 of text.

even the elements break free, as if tired of humans killing each other and to lay the field square; the Jhelum overflows and leaves for dead migrant refugees and rioters alike, unconcerned with religion. Friends become thirsty for each other's blood. Politicians, who conceived of these grand migrations, sit Tughlaq-like, Fikr says, as the transfers of population lead to the greatest misery, horror and bloodshed. *The Sixth River* is the evocative record and chronicle of the violent sixth river of passion that overwhelmed the Punjab with its brutal violence, or the river of blood that flowed as consequence of it, often merging with the five rivers of Punjab, its numerous canals, turning them red.

The Refugee Writes Back

Fikr's journal is a unique text in many ways. And in subsequent sections I seek to unravel its importance, as it became the reason for me to translate *Chhata Darya*. The foremost reason is the importance of *The Sixth River* as testimony and eyewitness account of Partition by a migrant and refugee, given on their own terms. Urvashi Butalia's seminal work that collected Partition testimony, *The Other Side of Silence* (1998), emphasized on how there 'is the generality of the Partition: it exists publicly in history books. The particular is harder to discover; it exists privately in stories told and retold inside so many households in

India and Pakistan' (4). Fikr's Partition text exists as an independent written record by a refugee that is outside both of Butalia's considerations, the post-event history written by Western or subcontinental scholars using archival records, and the important oral testimonies collected from refugees by not only Butalia but also Ritu Menon, Veena Das and others. *The Sixth River* is among the very few detailed records written during the Indian Partition but by a refugee in their own voice, and, in this case, one who was already a writer of note and an intellectual. It, therefore, retains the qualities of the reportage of events of the time, from an eyewitness and victim-participant position, but also with a literary verve.

There are other memoirs written, many by prominent politicians. To name but a few, there are Ram Manohar Lohia's *Guilty Men of India's Partition* and Maulana Azad's *India Wins Freedom* from India; and from Pakistan Jahanara Shanawaz's *Father and Daughter: A Political Autobiography* and Shaista Suhrawardy Ikramullah's *From Purdah to Parliament*. However, these often represent elite political concerns, or work primarily as political commentaries of events without capturing a common refugee's suffering personally. Anis Kidwai, activist, politician and later a member of the upper house of the Indian parliament, wrote her memoir in Urdu, *Azaadi ki Chhaon Mein*. It describes the Partition as experienced in Delhi, during her rehabilitation work with the refugee camps there. It has been translated into English by her granddaughter Ayesha Kidwai as *In Freedom's Shade* (2011). However, neither did Anis Kidwai migrate across the two countries, and nor was she a resident of a refugee camp herself. She had in fact been supported directly by Gandhi in her social work, following the death of her husband on government duty. She remains mostly adulatory towards Gandhi, and largely of the Congress. Moreover, her original text was also published much later, in 1974.

In contrast, *The Sixth River*, first published in 1948, within a year of Partition, is a memoir that captures the author's deeply felt and dearly held desire as a common man to not have to leave his beloved city, Lahore, that he held on to till November 1947, for about three months after the declaration of Lahore as belonging to Pakistan, the country created for the Muslims of India. These three months are a long time, when he is perhaps the only Hindu writer, if not professional, trying to go about his business to remain a part of the cultural, intellectual and professional life in Lahore, as rivers of blood and the fires of arson rage through it. Ultimately, Fikr is forced to migrate as a refugee, entering the camp at Lahore, then making the journey across Wagah on a lorry alongside other refugees, to reach the camp in Amritsar. This testimony of life over these three months in Lahore, ending with his migration to Amritsar, from the vantage point of a member of the intelligentsia, which was quite powerless at this time, thus acquires quite a unique status.

Moreover, not only is it one of the very few texts in Urdu or any other language written in the form of a Partition diary by a non-political leader, it is possibly the only non-fiction text written about Partition in such strongly satirical prose. Where a Saadat Manto is hailed as the master of the Partition short story genre, Fikr's *The Sixth River* predates all of Manto's works on Partition. And it is Fikr who is retelling his own story and that of other literary, political and everyday figures—victims, perpetrators and beneficiaries—with equal, possibly greater, irony.

And it is Fikr's style that further provides *The Sixth River* its harrowing potency. Fikr does not mince words, but crafts them with a surgical scalpel. Brevity is his forte, and in moments such as his own daughter's murder by his childhood friend, he recreates the impact of such trauma by eschewing sentimentality completely, and wielding his pen sparingly to describe the macabre in its bare outline. He ends up comforting the killer of his own child, almost reinventing notions of grief, mourning and consolation. Such was the impact of Partition on many that it produced previously un-thought responses, perhaps ones that even fiction could not have imagined or captured, and he shows the fortitude to think through them with inordinate calm.

His dark irony is counterbalanced by gentler, self-mocking and self-deprecating strokes in moments such as the opening diary entry where, after a bomb attack and some deaths, he laments not being able to have chai with his literary friends and discussing matters of culture. He also pokes fun at the newly converted who put on holy and pious airs out of fear and the need for survival, and laments the turning of the secular minds of some of his friends in the midst of the frenzy, while also dryly recording his anger and despondency at the abductions and rape of women, and sometimes the subsequent loss of any sense of shame in the face of brutality. Thus, Tarun Saint, in his essay on Partition memoirs, claims that *The Sixth River* 'appears as an atypical instance of testimony, not merely cataloguing and recording the moral debasement and horrors being witnessed, but rather registering grief, moral indignation and anger, emotions sublimated through the use of satirical barbs that unmask the pretensions of the community and political leaders intent on celebrating newly acquired independence.'* Astute political commentary and

---

*'Exorcising the Ghost of Times Past: Partition Memoirs as Testimony.' In *Revisiting India's Partition: New Essays on Memory, Culture, and Politics*. Ed. Amritjit Singh, Nalini Iyer, and Rahul Gairola. New York: Lexington Books, 2016. p. 84.

critique alongside the testimony are the third aspect that makes *The Sixth River* stand out in Partition literature.

Political Commentary and Critique

The seminal Urdu literary critic and translator, Muhammad Umar Memon, has asserted that the literature and 'fiction that emerged during and soon after the heat of the chaos of the Partition presents little more than variations on the all-pervasive theme of communal violence' (380).[*] *The Sixth River*, which has been remarked upon for its 'fictive' quality by Tarun Saint,[**] records much beyond the violence of the riot. Despite not being a trained historian, Fikr is able to step away from the immediate violence all around him to rationally interrogate causality. He is acutely conscious of global and local trends in politics, and critiques various political agents responsible for Partition and associated violence and conflict most insightfully.

Nehru, Jinnah, Gandhi—no major national leader escapes his ire for being unable to prevent Partition. Gandhi is chastised with deep resentment for offering to give up his life for the Punjab when Fikr feels that no one in the Punjab will be saved from death, even if

---

[*] 'Partition Literature: A Study of Intizar Husain.' *Modern Asian Studies*. Vol 14. Issue 3. July 1980, pp 377–400.

[**] op. cit. p. 85.

Gandhi died; especially after Gandhi had already done little to prevent Partition. Jinnah's speeches in English given to the masses are derided for their elitism. Nehru and Jinnah's ill-managed conception of the population transfer is obliquely derided, while their failure to relieve individual misery in tense situations of curfew is satirized.

Much of the blame is also thrown at the door of the British Empire: its hurried exit, Radcliffe's delayed and arbitrary line, and creation of conflict and Partition as a parting gesture and gift. Not only are the blasts described in the journal caused by bombs of English make, but Partition as strategy and legacy of British Empire is critiqued. The Joint Defence Council and The Boundary Commission are hauled up for their poor work. 'Buckingham Palace and [those propping up] Shivaji [are believed to] have signed a pact' (p. 93).

The princely states, and their dubious role in Partition violence is also remarked upon. The case of Patiala is commented upon at length, as the king claimed his army had reneged; an army whose 'former' members seemed to be complicit in violence, arson, pillaging and rape. The case of Kashmir and the opinions of Kashmiris, its Indian takeover, and the opinions of Pakistanis regarding a possible invasion—all feature in the form of discussions between numerous intellectuals, other citizens of Lahore, and newly arrived migrants from Kashmir or the new

India. Some of these discussions happen inside the (Communist) Party Office in Lahore, where Fikr is camped for safety, comfort and company in his final few days in Lahore.

Fikr contemplates joining the Communist Party in *The Sixth River*, but decides against it. We know that he did go on to join it in 1954 in India but quit within four years. In *The Sixth River* and elsewhere he also pokes fun at some writers, who were inspired by the socialist Progressive Writers' Movement in (Urdu) literature, for their political shortcomings and giving in to material gains and orthodox religious compulsions.

M.U. Memon argues that the writers writing on Partition could not interrogate the reasons behind Partition because almost all of them were under the influence of the Progressive Movement, which saw man as an a-cultural, utilitarian being, and therefore could see the religious division that was Partition only as destructive and meaningless. Fikr, while he admits to being influenced by the Progressive Movement, and may be regarded to be socialistic in many ways, is nonetheless critical of Progressive practice and proponents, often mocking himself for his failures as a Progressive. He describes some of his friends discussing the Partition and world politics in entirely socialist terms too. Fikr wishes to remind Rahi of his work with factory workers in Amritsar, and how the rulers and kings are fearful of their eventual rise. However, his own position in other moments is almost too individualistic to be preoccupied with Progressivism which may come at the cost of cultural and individual anonymity.

Fikr had also been allied with the Modernist group, Halqa-e-Arbab-e-Zauq or the 'Circle of the Men/Keepers of Taste', and therefore cannot be easily pigeonholed. And perhaps much more strongly than the Progressives, he retained a sense and sensitivity for the individual and their culture. Thus, even if like the Progressives, religion remains an almost an unimportant consideration for him, the cultural importance of Punjab reigns supreme.

Province over Country

Fikr's primary sense of loss, and the cultural identity or unit of belonging he wishes most strongly to hold on to, is the Punjab. It is this land of five rivers that is being torn asunder by the sixth river of destruction. It is this land of famous lovers such as Heer–Ranjha and Soni–Mahiwal, of saints such as Nanak, of folk song, and verdant fields, of inter-faith bonhomie, and intellectual stalwarts and poets such as Iqbal to which Fikr is wedded. Lahore in particular is his muse, his soulmate. He does not care for an India or a Pakistan. He makes his stand clear against this British cartographic exercise. Fikr does not care for the nation state. He has thrown his chips in with the weakest, with culture, with civilization. Not with ethnicity, not with religion. He is not quite articulating a federalism on the lines espoused by many minority or other national leaders of the time, but he certainly does not seem to care for the postcolonial state that is the remnant of Empire. Neither is Fikr interested in religion as a divisive force, being an atheist himself. The province of Punjab and city of Lahore is where he feels he belongs.

Non-Partisan Fikr

Even though Fikr is based in Lahore for most of the period described in *The Sixth River*, and much of the violence he sees directly and experiences personally is directed by Muslims against Hindus and Sikhs, Fikr never condemns any one religion. In fact, he sees hope in moments such as the burning of Bishan Das Building, where both Hindus and Muslims together are attempting to save copies of the Qur'an and the Hindu owner's son. Khwaja Nizamuddin, a Sufi *pir* or saint of Taunsa, who declares that if any Muslim harmed a Hindu he would curse all of them, and Gandhi, in the moment when he declares from Jama Masjid in Delhi after the Partition that he should first be killed before any Muslim is harmed, are heroes from across the newly made border. Most of his own (literary) friends are Muslims, and he does not feel anything particularly Indian as the nation state perhaps expects him to, and when a new citizen of India is visiting from Amritsar, he feels apathy.

Friends vs Nation

In 'What I Believe', E.M. Forster famously wrote that, if called upon, he wishes that he would have the strength to betray his country rather than betray his friend. Fikr consistently values his friendships far more than he values any other belonging, including that of the nation state. In today's milieu he might have been called an 'anti-national'. His affinity to his city of Lahore and the province of Punjab also arises out of his camaraderie, and his mutual regard for his fellow writer, editor, intellectual and artist friends such as Sahir Ludhianvi, Ahmed Rahi, Mumtaz Mufti, Qateel Shifai, Chaudhry Barkat Ali, and Arif Abdul Mateen. It is for the sake of these friends with whom he feels at one that he desires to stay in the city of Lahore, rather than to have to go to an alien India. He resists the migration for the longest time, but eventually gives in, when he feels betrayed by a close friend. And it is this ultimate betrayal that forces him to migrate.

Humanity in Evil or Evil in Humanity

Where Manto always showed humanity to arise even from the most evil of his characters, which was almost redemptive, Fikr's belief does not seem to ever be so sure. Perhaps this is due to the betrayals he felt he received. He does pick on instances that exhibit triumphs of humanity, a Jat Muslim family saving their Hindu neighbours, to name but one, still he does not leave for India with a happy heart. At the end the refugees protest saying they will not celebrate Diwali—Fikr had tried to warn them that the land they wished to claim as their own may be less welcoming than they think. It is not that he does not wish for humanity to progress, in fact he lends his voice of caution to this cause, in *The Sixth River*, and subsequent books and columns of satire. But skeptical satire is the best he can offer, not poetry. He wishes for improvement, but cannot rely upon it. If he goes looking to find humanity in all evil, he does not seem to shy from the evil that resides around the corner too. The question posed at almost the beginning and almost the end of *The Sixth River* is the same one on azadi, freedom. His milieu is looking for it in 1947, even after August. This search continues to resonate, and it must go on today for the sake of Fikr's spirit of humanism, but perhaps it ought to be also tempered with the self-conscious irony of his satire.

Maaz Bin Bilal
June 2019

Note on the Translation

Chhata Darya was first published (probably, since it is undated) in 1948. Two different editions of the original Urdu text of *Chhata Darya* have been referred to and collated to produce this translation. The first is the single-volume Naya Idaarah publication from Lahore (undated, from c. 1948). The second is from the Fikr Taunsvi special issue of the journal *Biswi Sadi* published in 1988. This second edition has numerous errors, which had to be corrected to derive the right meaning with the help of the first edition, which is of poorer production but of better editorial quality.

This translation has sought to recreate the mood and form of the original Urdu satire and irony as closely as possible in English. This was the key challenge as Fikr's style is fundamental to his expression and the gravitas he brings to bear upon his eyewitness account of and commentary upon Partition. Certain words from the original such as 'azadi' and 'malechha' were retained from the original Urdu for either their resonance in the subcontinental imagination today or their untranslatability. Others such as 'kaffir' are included in their Oxford English Dictonary form, as they have been accepted into English, sometimes with spellings that might seem odd to native speakers of Hindi-Urdu or Arabic from where these may arise. Certain sections that may appear somewhat opaque in the translation are also often so in the original Urdu, where Fikr remains intentionally indirect, and operates with extreme subtlety. Translating dark humour and irony are perhaps the greatest challenges for a translator, and I hope the losses here are not as great as the gains, for Fikr's *The Sixth River* deserves the wide audience that English may provide.

Maaz Bin Bilal
June 2019

Author's Dedication:
To the Five Rivers [of the Punjab]

Author's Note: This Diary

The Sixth River is the story of that barbaric time when human civilization was headed towards its acme with the help of science, philosophy, knowledge and literature; when nuclear man was breaking innumerable norms of tradition; and when two opposing religious traditions were colliding in India to lead to the bloodshed of millions of people.

Foreign rule had split the lively and verdant Punjab into two religious parts. Ten million people—having left their homes, fields, orchards, ploughshares, and loves and hates—were dragging their feet, wandering, fighting, burnt, cut up; many only to bite the dust. Innocent two-year-olds were picked up on the points of spears and flung into the air so that these sons of snakes would not grow up to bite the other faith. Modest young girls were paraded naked by those mothers' sons with the help of swords and lances so that these daughters of the Vedas, the Qur'an, and the Granth may nevermore give birth to man from their sacred wombs.

Therefore, man had reached that pinnacle of culture where he stood with his vain head held high at his own barbarity and bestiality. It is then that I wrote this story of blood and fire. The story revolves around those three months when—with the Partition of India, associated communal riots, and the transfer of population—the greatest mistakes in history were committed one by one. I spent those three months in Lahore, that Lahore which was the centre of high culture and civilization, which, with a single imperial blow, had been turned into the river of blood and fire. This river had soon spread to all corners of the beautiful and prosperous Punjab. And then some religious brutes rode its waves to play such a game of terror that history was horrified, philosophy was choked and the heart of science stopped beating.

In this diary, you will also find characters that emerge at appropriate moments in keeping with their unique qualities. They retain a representative place in the historical tragedy. Here feature the conservatives, religious believers, non-partisan participants, progressives, gossip-mongers, beasts, innocents, masked men and the main players of the time. If we look at them beyond their apparent personalities and locate them in their various social classes, then some confusion may be cleared and true meaning may be revealed.

Fikr Taunsvi
June 1948

The Sixth River

Journal from 9th August to 8th November 1947

In three parts:

- Mobbed by Darkness
- What Place Is This?
- Come, Let Us Look for the Dawn Again

Mobbed by Darkness

(Andhere ke Rele Mein)

9 August 1947

Last evening, a bomb had exploded in a cinema hall at Bhati Gate. They say it was a bomb of a foreign make, which is why fifty desis died with it. All those who died were Muslims. So, surely, the one who threw it had to be a Hindu, who had accomplished the seminal mission of decimating the malechha* Muslims with a bomb of English make, and an English heart and mindset. The bodies of the malechha were loaded in tongas and carried to the hospital. Someone had had half of his leg blown off, someone's skull had burst, and someone's intestines had poured out of their stomach, and people were running—from here to there, there to here. The bazaars closed down, the roads became desolate.

Arif and I could not have our daily tea today at Nazim Hotel.** Neither could we share 'learned' conversations on politics and literature, nor could we pour public art, science and philosophy down our

---

*Literally 'foreign', but used as a pejorative, often for Muslims in India who are considered invaders by conservatives.

**Arif Abdul Mateen (1923–2001), born in Amritsar, a poet and critic, who wrote in Urdu and Punjabi.

throats, along with swigs of hot tea. Today, Lahore's goons had paid due respect to the bangles sent from Amritsar. For, how could Lahore's brave goons accept this insult by Amritsar's brave goons: 'Ladies, wear these bangles and sit at home, this matter's beyond your prowess?'

Hence, the bravehearts couldn't stay indoors and took to the streets with bullets, bombs, pistols and swords. And within an hour of the bomb explosion, close to 150 cowards had been murdered in Lahore. Fifty houses had been burned down to ashes. The bazaars were emptied. Police had been posted to stand watch over the heart-wrenching spectacle of the burning houses. Army battalions and police troops with their trucks were loudly marching by to people the echoing and empty streets. The melancholic air was further leavened by shouts of 'Allahu Akbar' and 'Sat-Sri-Akal' the whole night. With red-red flames of fire and glowing sparks, the darkness of the night was illuminated.

Bomb explosions kept up, gunfire too went on. People were dying on the streets, the curfew continued, and the police kept up with its rounds, so that no man would dare break the law. Under the shade of mosques and temples, the proud and pretty ladies of dharma and mazhab were being kept safe. Mill and factory owners and landlords opened their coffers, so that any man who dared raise an eye towards our fair lady may be shot to death. One bullet—one dead—fifty rupees! One pellet, one dead, and sixty rupees! Two hundred and fifty rupees to anyone who throws a bomb. The price of a Kaffir, the compensation of a malechha. Human bodies were being sold for a cheap price in the market. Everyone was happy—the poor and the rich, the subjects and their king.

I could not get out of the house till ten this morning. I went on listening to the radio. Tried to forget myself in the sweet melodies of Shamshad and Saigal's records.* But my mind was so bogged down that it could find no rest in anything. The collection of Ghalib's poetry stared at me from the desk.** Einstein's *Principles of Relativity* went on snoring. Faiz's *Naqsh-i-Faryadi* screamed itself hoarse and grew quiet.† Mahatma

---

*Shamshad Begum (1919–2013) was one of the early female playback singers of Bombay cinema, and sang over 6,000 songs in Hindi, Bengali, Marathi, Gujarati, Tamil and Punjabi.

K.L. Saigal (1904–1947) was a singer and actor. He was initially based in Calcutta, then moved to Bombay with the industry.

**Mirza Asadullah Khan Ghalib (1797–1869): Arguably, the greatest Urdu poet, and considered to be the master of the ghazal form.

†Faiz Ahmed Faiz (1911–1984) was an MBE, Nobel nominee, Lenin Peace Prize-winning, Progressive Urdu poet, Marxist and lecturer in English. *Naqsh-i-Faryadi* is his first collection of poems published in 1941, and the title literally translates as the complainant's or dissenter's mark or impression.

Buddha's picture kept staring at me. Art, literature, philosophy, science—all were silent. All of them were dejected.

What was their grief? Was it different from the grief of the washerman who lived in the lower floor, and had a tiny-little child born to him at three last night? He was worried: the bazaars were closed, the milkman-sweet-seller had closed his shop and was skulking in a corner. He had not received milk at his shop today because it was brought by Muslim gujjars.* As this was a Hindu locality, they could not set foot here. And hospitals were closed; and doctors and nurses and midwives were gone. The washerman's newborn and his wife, who had just delivered, were both moaning and crying in pain, and the washerman was in despair.

'Sir, sir, will the curfew not be lifted? Will we not get milk?' In a state of anxiety, anguish and restlessness he had walked into my room. And I was looking towards Einstein, Mahatma Buddha, Ghalib and Iqbal: 'Tell him, tell him, respond to the washerman! What can you do to save his butter-soft child? Are you cheats? Have you been swindling us all this while? If you can't lift the curfew, if you can't bring the nurse to the washerman's house, then why did you give us this philosophy, this literature, this civilization, this

---
*Gujjars: A cattle-herding caste in north India.

knowledge? If only one of you were a Muslim gujjar who would come to the Hindu locality without ado. I wish you had the power to go and tell the great wits, those wise men, the prudent statesmen—Nehru and Jinnah—that, if only for a moment, they should take on this washerman's illiterate and plebian avatar. Only then should they go and tell the Englishman to give them independence, to give them India and Pakistan. Only then are they permitted to go and mix with the Labour leader Cripps, and with Mountbatten, and to organize conferences together. Tell them that we hate each other, and that we will strangle each other, even if this means that we won't have independence! But just as two swords may not be sheathed together in one case, two cultures will not live together in one country. Draw a line between us. Give us an order that you are divided. There the Hindu shall rule, here the Muslim will be sovereign; divide our rivers, divide our mountains, divide our Punjab. Split our Ravi and Beas,* sunder our Heer, divide our Sohni**—else we will chop each other to death and annihilation. And we won't let ourselves be independent—never!

---

*Ravi and Beas: Two rivers of the Punjab.

**Heer and Sohni are the female lovers from two of the most famous love stories of the Punjab, *Heer–Ranjha* and *Sohni–Mahiwal*.

But Mahatma Buddha and Gandhi remained silent. The washerman's eyes were filled with tears and Shamshad was singing, '*Saawan ke nazaare hain…*'

11 August

After the sickening and soul-wearying curfew of twenty-four hours, I finally stepped out of my house this morning. All around, some languid, dull activity had begun. Layers of terror and fear had accumulated over the roads. People were stepping gingerly over these layers. Doubt and fear—fear and doubt! It felt as if everyone on the road were carrying a bomb or a knife, and would bury it in the back of the enemy in the blink of an eye. All men kept turning around. Not men but foes walked that road. Hundreds of scared and hesitant enemies had stepped out of their homes. There were no friends among them. Ambling around, I eventually started up on the street leading to my office.

It stretched through a Muslim-majority area, where there had been a bomb blast three days ago. Going through these parts was a habit for me. It was a part of my mental make-up. What else could I have done? Mental peril lay in going through the safer parts. By the time I reached my office, smoke and flames had surrounded me. A grand building right next to the office was up in crackling flames. A large crowd was present. It was a curious mass—with Hindus and Muslims. Both were trying to douse the fire together.

The fire had united two cultures, two religions. I welcome such a fire, I salute it. I am ready to sacrifice millions of philosophical, learned and literary opinions and views on such a fire that allowed Muslims and Hindus a common torment on 11 August.

The first floor of the building read Bishan Das Building. The ground floor of the building housed a book-binder's shop, where scores of workers bound copies of the Qur'an daily. Both were burning—the Hindu building and the Muslim Qur'an. Some people were trying to recover the body of a seven- or eight-year-old boy buried under a girder on the first floor. Bishan Das's son was burning above as Muhammad's Qur'an burnt below. God's constitution was burning and Hindus and Muslims were dousing the fire together. A single scabbard was sheathing two swords.

I took great pleasure in the sight. Nowhere else in history had I found a reflection of such good taste. We were giving birth to a new history. I walked further. Ten paces away, in the middle of the road a decrepit, weak sixty-year-old man was sitting with his mouth open. His mouth and the side of his torso were bleeding. His open eyes, devoid of light, were staring at the sky. One soldier with a stick was guarding his life and limb. At the opposite square, shielded by five or six constables and one sub-inspector, rested the body of a thirty-year-old youth. By his side lay a bit of flour in a small bag, some of which had now spilt on the ground. The murderer had run away, because he had been in a hurry. He too probably wanted to dispose of three to four kaffirs and then take rest. He did not even wait for the police, but went away. And one soldier was saying: 'We have told these people so many times not to go through dangerous areas, but do they listen?'

The bag of the spilt flour was unable to answer the soldier's question. Locating Arif, I went into Islami Hotel at Bhati Gate for lunch. The hotel was noisier than usual. Some people were whispering while others were speaking in loud voices:

'We would cut these Sikhs into tiny pieces!'

'We will drink the blood of these Hindus!'

'We will kill each and every child of theirs!'

This passionate and wondrous storm was incredibly frightening. It had come to light that many lorries filled with hundreds of wronged soldiers and screaming and bawling Muslims had arrived in Lahore today. The officers of Amritsar had released the Muslim soldiers as they had now gotten Pakistan, and according to the officers the soldiers could no longer remain in the bondage of the service of the Hindus. Their weapons had been snatched away from them. And they had run away with their lives to Lahore. They had spread to every street and alley. And Lahore's streets were now overrun with a flood. A flood of blood, a storm of fire.

A Maulvi Saheb with a salt-and-pepper beard said: 'Oh, God Almighty! Did you hear? Lahore has witnessed about a hundred and twenty incidents of murder today. This city is headed for its doom this day.'

Arif was getting nervous. He was now worried about my safety. Suddenly, the hotel started to close down. People got up and ran. A crowd was passing by on the street shouting slogans. A lorry was also screeching along: 'Curfew has been imposed again in Lahore from 12 o'clock. Ninety-hour curfew.' I said to Arif: 'This time the number of curfew hours has been increased because the count of crimes has also gone up. Crime and curfew are obviously inseparable. That flour sack unnecessarily comes in the way to complicate matters.'

I went towards Anarkali.* The very thought of going home again to be imprisoned weighed heavy. Many great Indian poets and writers were coming out of the Mall Square coffee house, as I reached it. Their literature or art was not more exalted than the curfew. That is why they were running to their homes in a restless and troubled state: Bari, Salahuddin, Yusuf, Mittal. In his distinctive manner, Mittal said to me: 'Tell me, Fikr, my friend, will you come to India? I am going.'

---

*Famous bazaar in Lahore.

I replied: 'The curfew has started. You go home first. It is only after n-i-n-e-t-y hours that you will be able to leave this country of free men. Go, go home quickly.' I came away wondering in which direction was the Progressive artist headed?*

My head was exploding. I had nearly passed out by the time I neared Rehbar's place.** Comrade Rehbar had left a few days back, and his words were still echoing in my head: 'Brother, I am leaving. I will come again, I will come again.' His tone was full of guilt. I had retorted in exasperation: 'Go, comrade, go.' Then instead of going home I went to Jagdish's place.†

Uff! It felt as if hammers were being struck on my head. The nerves were taut, as if they would snap any moment to render my frame lifeless. Accidents and encounters were unravelling today in a fast and continually spiralling chain of events, which shackled

---

*Progressive: The Progressive Writers' Movement of the Anjuman Taraqqi Pasand Musannifeen-i-Hind was a Left-leaning and anti-imperial writer's movement that began with Sajjad Zaheer's edited collection of short stories *Angarey* (1932), which included stories by him, Rashid Jahan, Ahmed Ali and Mahmud-uz-Zafar, and was banned by the colonial Indian state the following year.

**Rajendra Nath Rehbar (b. 1931) was an Urdu poet of both the ghazal and nazm forms, and Hindi-film lyricist. His poems have been composed to music and sung by Jagjit Singh, among others.

†Jagdish Rai: A well-off friend with a Hindu background with an interest in Urdu poetry.

me, as I writhed underneath its weight. Jagdish had still not come. His servant was packing the bags and piling them up in the courtyard. It turned out that Jagdish had gone to arrange for a truck. He is leaving. Jagdish is also leaving. This fan of Iqbal, who is in love with Islam, this poet, this poet of Urdu, is leaving. Mittal is leaving, Rehbar is leaving, Kapoor is leaving. And sleep hits me now—free of bomb explosions, more potent than ricocheting bullets, carefree of fleeing poets and writers.

12 August

I fled Jagdish's house. He was in a strong state of agitation and difficulty despite his learned demeanour and writerly tone. I could sense fear in his condition. He said: 'It is not possible for me to stay here anymore, Fikr bhai! I have loved this city all my life. But...but, this city is now running up to claw me. Many lorries filled with injured and dead Muslims have come in today from Amritsar. And ever since their arrival in Lahore, they have stoked the fires of revenge. Go, look! Look: all the Hindus of Lahore are being slaughtered like goats and sheep! And are turning up to gather in droves at the camps. No one will live here now. Not me, not you. Yes! No one! Where will you go? Come, let's go to India! Come?'

I replied: 'I am going to Multan!'

'Multan!' He looked at me with extremely

incredulous eyes. 'You'll go to Multan? Arey, Multan has gone to Pakistan! Are you a fool? Have you lost your head? There is mayhem at the station. Hundreds have been killed there since morning. And you are going to Multan! Okay, okay, tell me, will you buy this radio set of mine?—this bed?—this almirah? Give! What will you pay for all this? Hundred rupees? Is that fine?'

And I fled from Jagdish's house. Like a mouse flees a cat's grasp. Jagdish had set up shop: tell, tell, what will you buy? Will you buy Lahore? Buy the waves of the Ravi? Eight annas per wave. The Samadhi of Ranjit Singh? Ten annas per brick. Sitla Mandir? Six annas per statue. Mall Road? A rupee for a furlong. Say, what will you buy?

What do I do? I cannot live in these maddening surroundings. On all the roads of Sant Nagar, people burdened with their beddings, trunk cases and baggage were running away in droves. I closed my eyes. Put fingers in my ears. A few Hindu boys had broken into a Muslim vegetable-vendor's shop, and were picking up bananas, guavas and oranges and throwing them in the drain. They were guffawing and singing. They were swaying with intense happiness and joy. I went ahead with my head bowed. Kept moving and passing them by, slowly, slowly. Kept walking, slowly. Perhaps, I was headed towards my home. Or maybe I was headed towards the refugee camps. Or was going towards

Mall Road. Perhaps, I was headed to the Coffee House to have a cup of coffee. Maybe, I...maybe, I... The Coffee House was closed. Today, Lahore's writers, poets, political commentators, philosophers and historians could not step out of their houses. So the Coffee House was closed. And then, the number four omnibus appeared like a miracle with delightful possibilities and parked in front of me. I scrambled to get in; without thinking, without looking where that bus was headed, and when it would leave.

The bus stopped at Regal Cinema. The dangerous areas lay ahead.

14 August

What a strange day it was. It weighed on my mind the whole night. That diminutive, thin storyteller remains stuck to my mind's membrane like a lizard. I do not wish to try to flick him away. Because he is very interesting. I am interested in his complicated, unclear movements. When he speaks it feels as if he has Plato hidden in the depths of his soul. But explicitly he makes convoluted conversations to tangle me up. Irritation borders on annoyance. But I find that confusion, that irritation pleasurable. Because he accepts his defeat in everything. But despite that defeat his Plato is unable to attain Nirvana. Actually, he is a little weird, like the evening fog blended into night.

And yesterday when the evening fog blended

into the night, I was wandering on that desolate, uninhabited and dangerous street with complete abandon, foolishness and lack of fear. So, he couldn't even believe my presence there. He had stared at me, groping in an attempt to gather what this person, this spindly, thin man—who would be driven senseless at hearing the roar of any Muslim goon, whose mahatmaness, whose art, whose poetry, and greatest of all, whose religion, could all be terminated in a jiffy—was doing on this street filled with danger, in the middle of this fire- and blood-spewing storm, roaming around with a foolhardy bravado? As if his death could not protect Islam?

Death, terrible death—in the lanes of Lahore, on the streets, in the bazaars, at the corners, on windows, in Hindus, in Muslims, in Sikhs—stalks everywhere. But perhaps death's satanic eyes did not fall upon this skinny little poet. Or maybe he walks into the face of death, towards its eyes with such a lack of care that death starts to blink its eyes. You? You? Who are you? Who *are* you? Do not come towards me like that. Those about to die do not come this way. Don't you know the ways to enter the company of death? Go away, go away. Get out of my sight. You fool, go! Wander in the streets, ramble through the lanes. I cannot understand you, what is your name, what is your creed? People of your faith are not worthy of becoming victims of the bloody reign of this bestiality, this barbarity and monstrosity. Go, whom do you seek here? Do you wish to meet Mumtaz?* Do you believe him? This Muslim? Have his Islamic honour and self-respect died that he won't stab you even once with his knife? A knife can kill twenty to twenty-five, even thirty to forty, people. A knife can show 240 million gods the way to redemption and peace. A knife can kill the awakened Islam of 70 million people. A knife can...you are a strange man!

Yes—seeing a strange man like me with his face turned up to the sky made Mumtaz tremble all over. Like the sharp edge of a sword, lines of sweat were making deep cuts on his forehead as they crawled along.

'Oh, it's you!'

'Yes, it's me,' I said nervously.

'Where are you going? Don't go! On the way, on the way is that terrible area where there was firing, rat-a-tat gunfire, the whole night. Don't you go there in the dark.' He had tried to counsel me without pausing for a thought, scared as he was.

'Actually, yaar,' I had started walking with him,

---

*Mumtaz Mufti (1905–95) was born in Batala, now in Indian Punjab. He was in Lahore at the time of Partition and stayed on as a Pakistani citizen. Mumtaz was a short-story writer, initially inspired by liberal European intellectuals such as Freud before being attracted by Sufism, and finally becoming a patriotic Pakistani.

'I am unable to stay in Sant Nagar anymore. I will die there without any due reason. My brain will explode. I am not here to go, but I have come. I will stay with you, till the time you do not forget the etiquette to keep me safe. I feel smothered there in that environment. All Hindus live there. All gods. And gods are running away. Leaving their homes, their yards, their neighbourhoods, their affections, their hatreds, their habits, their emotions, even themselves. They are running away—why? Why are they running away, Mumtaz? Would their running away douse the fires of these blazing buildings? Will these bombs that burst night and day, these bloodied humans, and these slogans—these sky-splitting slogans, and these slogans that rip into the hearts of bhagwan and khuda—will these also run away? Tell me, Mumtaz! I can't grasp anything. Should I also run away? But where? I don't even know this art of fleeing. When I try to escape I cannot find my way among the many paths. Does the path lead to your house? You—who are born in the house of a Mussulman, you walk on this path every day, you are not scared in the least of walking on this route. And I...I forget the way to my house and follow the path to yours—is this path false? Are you familiar with its destination, Mumtaz? Are you?'

And I continued to deliver an illogical, absurd, aimless and meaningless, confused and rambling lecture. Managing to sway their minds. He brought me to his sitting room and sat me down. Threw a pack of cigarettes and a box of matches at me. I threw the back of my head on the chair, spread my legs, put my feet up on the charpoy opposite and started taking long drags. He went in to arrange tea for me. And then he kept thinking, thinking, thinking, 'What idiocy!' But apart from this idiocy, this fear, what option did he have? 'You are safe now. Don't worry about anything. Nobody can cast an evil eye upon you here.' He kept assuring me while serving me tea. And I kept listening to him while drinking tea. And eventually asked, 'Mumtaz, what do you think of the philosophy of Confucius?'

What a strange day. It still prevails on my mind.

15 August

All of last night, the radio kept shouting: azadi, azadi, azadi!

Today we are free of foreign rule. Mumtaz is happy that our politics has finally gotten off the fence and has chosen a side. Early in the morning, I entered his room with an anguished look on my face: 'Do you know, Mumtaz, that we have been free since 12:01 a.m., but firing still went on all night? Allahu Akbar, Har Har Mahadev and Sat Sri Akal are still in prison, and they have protested all night by shouting, echoing and jumping around, as if to say that we do not wish to be free, we wish to remain alive. We will die if we are freed.'

I do not know what had happened to me in that moment. It felt as if I had been swimming in a pool of poison all night. Sarcasm, barbarity and hatred were erupting like sparks out of each of my body parts. And I was humming:

'What place is this? Where have you stopped?'

He asked me: 'Are you sad with independence?'

But I kept humming that same line as if by habit.

'Come, let us welcome freedom together,' he supplied me with hollow consolation.

'Yes, yes. Mumtaz, you are right. We should welcome this nymph together. With mounds of the corpses of Hindus, Muslims and Sikhs, with bomb explosions and burning buildings we should welcome her. Didn't you hear—Delhi and Karachi both became brides last night? With drums, shehnai, dance and sarod music, they went on celebrating their wedding. This was their wedding night. And we, our Lahore, our Punjab, Sohni's pot and Heer's bangles,* and our flowing farms had presented as gifts our innocent children, our

---

*In the love story of Sohni–Mahiwal, Sohni would use a clay pot as a float, with the help of which she would swim across the river to meet her lover, Mahiwal. A jealous relative found out about this and replaced the clay pot with a half-baked one, leading to Sohni's death by drowning. Together with Heer's bangles as adornments (Heer was also poisoned by a relative just before her scheduled marriage with Ranjha who then too consumed the poison knowingly), Sohni's pot becomes a powerful symbol of the (tragic) love of the Punjab.

young girls, our greyed and wizened elderly and our sharp youths for this auspicious occasion.'

'Will you have tea?' Mumtaz asked, exasperated by my emotional speech. His eyes seem to wonder: from where has such venom gotten inside this man? Why is he hiding reality behind a veil of emotions? This is the reality, and it cannot be wiped out by glistening tears. Maybe he was thinking that I must hate that happiness which that youth had experienced by flying the Crescent Flag at the Secretariat. Would he hate in this way? No, no! Maybe, it wasn't so. Maybe, he didn't hate this happiness. Maybe, maybe—his mind was in a whirl again. Why couldn't Mumtaz probe into my hatred? Mumtaz, who had a Masters in psychology, who knew the secrets of human hearts, why couldn't he understand me?

He was starting to believe that I was a fool.

'Fool! What a great fool, I am, Mumtaz! All of India is dancing in bliss, singing songs of happiness and joy. But these waves of happiness—why have they died in me? Tell me the cause of their death, Mumtaz!' I was staring unblinkingly at the ceiling.

But where was the cause of the death of these waves hiding inside me? I had asked Mumtaz this amidst our conversation the previous day. Yesterday, on the road to Ichhra, I had witnessed a jolting scene.*

---

*Ichhra is a neighbourhood in Lahore with a famous, old bazaar.

An excited crowd was gathered with sticks in hand, in front of a place of worship. Outside that place of worship, rotten burnt bodies of worshippers were being piled on a lorry. In the morning, the burly army men had arrived to rescue these dead bodies. And now they were pulling them out of the burnt monument and throwing them into the truck. As if sacks of freshly made jaggery were being loaded.

Both of us did not leave the house the whole day. Today, on the day of Independence, we remained imprisoned in the house. Something would repeatedly get stuck in my throat. We kept drinking tea the whole day. Mumtaz kept saying: 'Come, let's go for a stroll outside.'

Today, all monuments would be flying the flags of the independent nations, Union Jacks would be taken down. People would be ecstatic, celebrating the joy of freedom with great enthusiasm. But my feet were as if they had forgotten how to walk. My eyes were growing dark. I couldn't look at this frenzy, this zeal, this passion. What frenzy was this that had no joy nor jouissance? What wine was this that was not intoxicating? What song was it that was brimming over with men? Turn off this song. Don't strike this harp. And sleep, all of you sleep. Shut your eyes, and let the Joint Defence Council stand guard.* Let the Boundary Commission stay awake and keep watch.** So that when your eyes open you can see nine million people soaked in blood. Settlements razed to the ground, ruined cities, burnt fields and dry rivers can welcome you when you are awake. And the guards would have left. After your eyes have opened, what need will be there for the guards to take any trouble?

---

*On 22 July 1947 it was decided that the Partition Council would function as the Provisional Joint Defence Council (JDC) until 15 August 1947, when the latter would come into being. The JDC was set up by the Joint Defence Council Order on 11 August 1947 and was valid up to 1 April 1948. It consisted of the Governor-General of India as Independent Chairman, the Defence Ministers of India and Pakistan and the Supreme Commander. The JDC was to oversee the division of the Indian forces between the Dominions and their reconstitution as two separate Dominion forces, among other defence-related matters.

**The Boundary Commission was a consultative committee created in July 1947 to recommend how the Punjab and Bengal regions of the Indian subcontinent would be divided between India and Pakistan shortly before each was to become independent from Britain. The commission—appointed by Lord Mountbatten, the final viceroy of British India—consisted of four members from the Indian National Congress and four from the Muslim League and was chaired by Sir Cyril Radcliffe. The commission's mandate was to draw boundaries in the two regions that would keep intact as much as possible the most-cohesive Hindu and Muslim populations within Indian and Pakistani territory, respectively. As the 15 August Independence date loomed and with little chance for agreement in sight between the two sides, Radcliffe ultimately made the final determination on the frontiers (from *Britannica*).

From the lower floors of the house, loud cries and sobs could be heard. Mumtaz told me that a family clan had arrived from Amritsar. Two children, both five years old, one young girl of seventeen and one old man—from a family of fifteen, only they had survived. Oh, my god!

17 August

For two days, the most frightening and horrifying news has been pouring in. Since getting Independence, contrary to expectation and hope, we could not sit in peace. Lahore and Amritsar have spread the flames of their fires to the east as well as the west. Twelve districts have been declared riot-ridden and been handed to the safety of the English Captain's watch, because the representatives of the independent governments can't excuse themselves from their joyous celebrations. They have no doubt about the Englishman's integrity. One who doubts that race which has released from its hands the golden bird that is India is indeed a troublemaker.

And the English captain could not see Punjab's composite culture dying. Therefore, he has appointed Hindu-Sikh military in Muslim-dominated areas and Muslim military in Hindu-Sikh-dominated areas so that this independent force of an independent country can execute their missions with full freedom. But despite his honest and honourable execution and practice, there is news that is horrifying and frightening.

News comes, bodies come. The injured come in

hordes. Screaming and crying, people come. Why these bodies, these injured, this screaming and shouting? They say the soldiers are destroying the goons. The Muslims feel that this murder and loot, destruction and barbarity have been started by Hindu and Sikh thugs. And Hindus and Sikhs feel that the onus for this loot lies squarely with the Muslim goons. So now, obligations and responsibilities increase on both sides. And along with responsibilities, the body count grows as well. We have arrived in the dark ages. English politicians and counsellors are of the opinion that till the time you gentlemen will not turn towards the days of the Stone Age, you will not attain true nirvana or redemption, nor the complete joys of freedom.

Today, neither in the morning nor in the afternoon did the radio broadcast that congratulatory soul-warming news for which all of Punjab—the looted, maimed and slain Punjab—was waiting with bated breath. Radcliffe's decision was still safe.* The line was concealed in this decision. That snake was hidden here which would uncoil its long thin body amidst Kalidasa's springs,**

---

*Sir Cyril Radcliffe's demarcation line between India and Pakistan was announced or published only on 17 August 1947, two days after the independence of India, with its citizens unsure of whether the place they were in would go to Pakistan or India.

**Kalidasa (c. 4th-5th C CE) was a classical Sanskrit playwright, famous for plays such as *Abhijnanasakuntalam*, which were often romantic comedies.

Waris Shah's Heer,* Iqbal's Selfhood,** Tagore's *Gitanjali*, and Mir's† and Ghalib's ghazals. And it will tell them: 'Turn your faces that way, look here, look there. Your share of meat lies there, and yours there. Identify your share, and tear into them. Gobble them up.' And those struck by hunger were waiting for it anxiously, but the snake was trapped in Radcliffe's basket.

Where had this snake come from? Do you know Mumtaz? Have you heard that speech by Churchill that he made at the dance-theatre of the puppeteers about the two pieces of the meat of independence being thrown to India: 'This proposal by the Labour government will be written in the annals of history in golden letters.' And upon hearing this speech, Churchill's past had started unravelling before my eyes. Darkness, darkness, only darkness—the Atlantic

---

*Waris Shah (1722–1798) was a Punjabi Sufi saint of Chishti order, who wrote *Heer*—the doomed romance of Heer and Ranjha.

**Iqbal (1877–1938), Sir Mohammad Iqbal or Allama Iqbal, was a major Urdu poet, who worked with German philosophy alongside an Islamic nationalism to come up with the concept of khudi or selfhood. He had asked for a self-ruling Muslim dominion within India, and has been hailed as mufakkir-i-Pakistan or the thinker (sometimes spiritual father) of Pakistan.

†Mir Taqi Mir (1723–1810) is hailed as the greatest of Urdu poets alongside Ghalib.

Charter!* And Churchill was happy at this darkness. Our benefactors were happy. And Gandhi was sitting in Calcutta, begging for peace.** And the alms-giving donors had spread to each and every city, town and village of the Punjab, and were making the foolish slaves aware of their freedom by the jabs of their spears, burning down the huts and the settlements, and throwing the [former] slaves out of their farms, their homes and their neighbourhoods.

Worn down, Mumtaz and I came out of the house. On the streets and at the shops, Crescent flags of freedom were flying. But it seemed as if they were looking up to the sky in appeal. In the flapping of the flags, any joyous song was missing. Their waving did not have the intoxicated and fearless flight of the Union Jack. People gathered in small groups on the street were whispering to each other. There was defeat in those whispers—sadness and tiredness. As if their long faces were saying: 'What's the use? What's the use?' Young children were selling tiny little flags:

'One flag for one anna!'

'My flag is good, sir!'

---

*Atlantic Charter: Signed between Franklin D. Roosevelt and Winston Churchill on 14 August 1941, was the declaration of the U.S. and British War aims, and the Allied goals for the post-war world.

**Gandhi had been present in Calcutta, along with the local Muslim leader, Shaheed Suhrawardy, on the eve of Independence to broker peace between the rioting Hindus and Muslims.

'No, mine!'

'No, mine!'

A group of boys had gathered around us. Mumtaz quickly bought a flag. I asked: 'What's the use?' He replied: 'We would be authenticated as Muslims this way. Genuine Muslims. No thug will doubt us anymore.' 'All right, all right,' I mumbled. And the flag boy lurched towards the bidi shop with the one anna we gave him. 'Right, right,' I mumbled, 'the free nation's free boy—one flag, one drag of a bidi. One flag, the Islamic movement proven right. So, was this flag proving the Islamic movement right? What?—this flag?' I stroked the flag waving from the cycle with affection and said to Mumtaz, 'Mumtaz, I will be a most faithful citizen of Pakistan—right? And have you heard? The tricolour was not allowed to be hoisted from the Amritsar District Court. Because this insulted Guru Nanak. The god of virility and of the virgin. In the Guru's city, only the Guru's flag could be hoisted.* This tricolour? It is the fad of Hindus, Muslims, Sikhs, Christians, Untouchables, and who knows how many other riffraff races. But the Guru's flag is nobler than any of them—the flag of faith, religion's flag, the flag of Hinduism, the Sikh flag, the flag of Muslims.

Anarkali felt like a corpse. It lay prostrate, unheeding, lifeless like a cadaver. Sad and depressing.

---

*Guru's Flag: the Nishan Sahib is the Sikh triangular flag with a saffron base and a black symbol of the Khanda on top.

One building was still on fire. They say that that building had goods worth lakhs of rupees—of a Hindu businessman, who would often get arrested on charges of black marketing, only to be released later. Right opposite, a Muslim trader's grand shop had been burnt to ashes. They say that this Muslim trader had also earned lakhs of rupees in the black market during the War.* On a half-burnt wall of this building, a poster was still stuck: 'This building is now the property of Pakistan.' A thug sitting at the paan store with a topi perched at an angle on his head had begun staring at us with doubtful eyes.

'Assalam-o-alaikum,' Mumtaz said going up to the paan-seller. 'Make me a paan, please.' Tilted topi looked at us with disappointment in his eyes, and went away waving its stick.

The clock at Anarkali Chowk had gotten stuck at five past seven. Time had stopped. Its feet were stuck. The pendulum was silent, and forlorn. Maybe it was ruminating upon something. Maybe it was wondering about what had happened? The handcuffs of the centuries-old captives were finally off. They were free to indulge in the macabre dance of blood and fire. It was amazed at how this could be so. Maybe history had made a mistake. Maybe time could not keep pace with it. And had gone ahead without a say in the matter.

---

*Probably referring to the Second World War.

The grand and majestic temple next to the square was burning. Unabatedly, unabashedly. And there was no one to prevent it. Clouds of smoke were rising and getting dispersed in the air. Scores of gods were trapped inside. Krishna, Ram, Shivji, Parvati and Hanuman had all been burnt away. *Manu Smriti*, *Rig Veda*, *Ramayana* and Shaastra had been consumed. They had taken flight from the prison of materiality. Everyone had been released from house arrest and the grand priest had fled. And with him, also his lovers and his devadasis. A very big statue of Hanuman lay in four pieces in the courtyard. How brave was Hanuman. It is said that as a child he fell from the air and crashed into a heavy rock, but did not get hurt at all. How valiant, what a lionhearted boy—he was now lying in the yard in four pieces.

The rising smoke had the fragrance of sandalwood. Today was the day of the sacrifice of gods in human rituals. I asked the soldier snoozing at the grand entrance to the temple: 'So, will the priest of this temple never return now?' The soldier's mouth was left hanging: 'Sir, please don't joke, let's chant the name of God.' And Mumtaz and I tried to remember God by lighting up our cigarettes.

Beyond the temple, a long row of houses was dancing to the tune of a blazing fire. It felt as if homes had gotten used to arson. As if it had entered their daily duties. 'Now, even two words of commiseration don't escape the lips when looking at these burning homes, Mumtaz. If homes must burn, then they should burn every third day, twice a week, but daily? Daily? No charm survives this way!' And Mumtaz grabbed my arm and pulled me away. He had perhaps seen the poisonous tears brimming inside me. And he started worrying for my life. He was sure that if this poison kept spreading inside me, then one day, one day...

Mumtaz bought another flag for an anna on the way back. It was necessary to safeguard life.

19 August

Radcliffe announced his award. Bengal's culture, art, dance and music were divided. Punjab's ploughs, farming, songs and romance had been carved up. One aspect of this division was really curious: both Muslims and Hindus were dissatisfied with this. But what is the use of their dissatisfaction? This was an act of fate. And fate lay in the hands of Radcliffe. A few serious-minded people were calling this emotional dissatisfaction meaningless. Because the leaders had agreed to abide by the verdict even before it was ever given. Mumtaz bought a map from the market. The map of Punjab. And while listening to the verdict on the radio he drew a line on the map. He was drawing a snake. A thousands-of-miles-long snake. And the snake had thrown his birthplace Batala into India. His face was livid. I could see millions of glowering faces in his flushed face. Faces that were protesting, that were shouting:

'Why was our birthplace not included in Pakistan?'

'Our birthplace should have been included in India!'

Millions of faces were livid, smarting and disappointed. But the snake had been sent by Brahmaji. And Brahmaji was interested in neither Mumtaz nor Batala. He was only interested in obeying the will of God.

'This is a big conspiracy.' It was as if a great wave of tears had risen in Mumtaz's throat and wanted to come out now. And he was shouting himself hoarse, loudly informing the verdict and its repercussions to all the other gents of the neighbourhood. And getting all tied up in knots inside. He was wondering how Batala, with a population of 80 per cent Muslims, could go to India.

'This is injustice, this is sheer tyranny. This can never happen...'

The artist's—Mumtaz's—veins had become taut. He was fidgety. Looking at his face one perceived a trace of fear. And I was trying to think of means to allay that fear. I wanted to pick him up from this small world and throw him into a cosmopolitan world. 'Here, here, Mumtaz; come out of the shell of your Batala. This is a common grief, not yours alone. You are an individualistic artist.

But who cares about individuality anymore? The world is rapidly getting divided into two camps. The globe has come to a crossroads in its perambulations. And the astrologers are keenly observing its path. They are trying to predict its revolutions. The division of Pakistan and India and their new existence are only one part of these revolutions. Who are you? What is your Islam? What is my Hinduism? Nothing. We are but pawns, my dear! The player places us where he wants. Nankana is kept in Pakistan, Batala in India.* Both pawns are shouting: "We will overturn this game! We will not allow this game to continue. This is tyranny, this is injustice." But, Mumtaz, the game goes on. It will reach its conclusion. Look, look, do you see that spark?—that flame which grants the same light to Arabia and Himalaya, to China and Egypt, to Batala and Nankana; the same passion, the same pain! And look, look into that light, in the tangled darkness, in the growing dark, how we are being looted.'

But Mumtaz had already climbed down. His restlessness and anguish had the capacity to break his mind. I kept calling out to him, again and again, 'Mumtaz! You should go take a cold shower, or you'd go mad! This is the age of madness. Madness, terror, and barbarity fly in the air with their wings spread

---

*Nankana: Birth place of the founder of Sikhism, Guru Nanak.

wide. See, if that piece of your heart Achha,* and your mother who birthed you, and your relatives are all in Batala, and Batala is caught in the wilderness of India, and if India is ruled by the savage Sikhs, goons, and beasts, what can you do about it? If my wife and daughter are in Pakistan, then what can I do? What happened? What *happened*? Look at me. I am sitting calmly, reading Iqbal, referring to Goethe. And my skull is about to explode. My nerves and sinews are hyperactive. Still I am content. I see no sign of enslavement in the Radcliffe line. You will surely find your dear and beloved Achha. If you have firm belief and faith in the purity and holiness of love then you will surely find Achha. You will surely find Achha, Mumtaz!'

But Mumtaz had left. And I had been lecturing into the void. The servant came back to tell me that he had gone looking for the lorry: 'I do not know what will happen now, sir; Mr Mumtaz is acting crazy.'

He did not return till the evening. My anxiety had increased. I would laugh, I'd smile, and suddenly become quiet. I had traversed the expansive oceans of silence but seen no shores. Everywhere I saw was a hullabaloo, fighting and storms. Blood, blood, blood! Fire, fire, fire! And this fire had spread in all directions. From cities to the villages, from councils to farms, in huts and settlements, its flames were to be seen.

---

*Achha is the son of Mumtaz.

All of Punjab is burning. The flame has reached Achha's brow in Batala. In Taunsa, my wife's sari is catching fire from the crackling blaze. I have reached my village. My daughter reaches the house of Ali Mohammed Butt as she plays. And Ali Mohammed has picked her up and dashed her on the ground with real force. Her soft, delicate bones are broken into bits. Ali Mohammed is my childhood friend and companion. We used to play gilli-danda together in the colony. He is a big landlord in the settlement now, and writes letters full of affection to me. He has brought the body of my dead daughter to my house.

'Forgive me, my friend. I did not break this branch. A harsh and rapid gust of wind came, and she broke with a snap to fall into my yard.' His eyes are wet with tears. There is uproar in the village. Clack, clack, clack. Possibly, the Masudi clan had attacked the village once again. And Hindus and Muslims are combating them together. Maybe, the Hindu-Sikh military has started gunning down the Muslims, and the Muslims have started firing at the Hindus.

My daughter lies dead on the ground. And Ali Mohammed is handing his six-year-old son to me: 'Fling him, Fikr bhai, dash him hard on the ground, such that my sins may be forgiven! My heart may come to rest and I stand punished. Dash him, dash him, my friend!' I hugged the little rose-like Rashid to my heart. 'Go away, go away, Ali Mohammed, you have gone mad. Why don't you get yourself treated? Go, go, I will not give Rashid to you. Rashid, my son!'

25 *August*

For the past four or five days, I feel as if I have been hung in mid-air, like someone spending their life in dream-world. So many jolting, sombre and severe realities are presenting themselves from all sides. But I do not wake up from my sleep. Mumtaz has not met me for four days. I am straying in the dark. Mumtaz is straying in the dark. All creation is crashing around like whirlwinds in the overwhelming darkness of the abyss.

I try my best to focus myself on a single worldview but everything is slipping through my fingers. I cannot grasp anything. If I had airplanes then I would drop bombs like rain on these goons who kill innocent people on trains. The bloodied trains then reach Lahore Station, and the platforms get covered with mounds of corpses. And then groups of Muslim mujahideen attack Hindu-Sikh trains passing through Pakistan to cover in human blood the platforms of Amritsar, Jallandhar and Ludhiana, so that the people of India do not think of them as shameless cowards. What madness is this? Oh, why don't I wake up from my sleep? Why doesn't Mumtaz wake up? Why don't Jinnah and Jawahar bat an eyelid? Now, Pakistan and India even have two independent governments. The people want these governments to prosper. And the people are with their leaders, ready to lose their heads on their orders. Then these people, these citizens, why are they losing their heads without the orders of their leaders? The leaders have not told them: go kill each other, ruin your settlements. Throw the Hindu out of Pakistan, don't let the Muslim remain in India. Where has this face of hatred come from? Its features and countenance don't appear to be human. Then? Then? What do these people want? Only to fight? To fight without a purpose? It is almost ten days since Independence. But even after gaining independence they are still fighting a war. It belies understanding. It is a subversive and insidious flood of hatred which is sweeping everyone away. A sea of blood that is leaping and spilling over everyone's head.

Mumtaz leaves the house every morning. He is looking for a lorry that would bring his beloved Achha, his mother and sisters and his relatives from Batala to Lahore. But every evening he comes back with a long face, disappointed. Because the Pathan lorry owner is asking for one thousand rupees. One thousand rupees!* But Mumtaz has no money. And

---
*Equivalent to approx. 3,00,000 rupees or £3,000 today. Conversion by using approximate rate of 1£=13 rupees in 1947 and then converting the pounds to the 2018 value using inflation calculator from www.bankofengland.com.

his Achha is waiting for him in Batala. Achha is the memento of his previous love. And love has become a commodity, and the traders are earning thousands a day. They have brought love to the market and are selling it off. Mumtaz comes to this market every day. His love is imprisoned in the lorry of the Pathan, who seems to make a face at Mumtaz each day to tease him: 'Cough up the money if you want to buy Achha! What do you have? A book of stories? A collection of essays on sexuality? Freud and Adler's psychological analyses? Art for life? Art for art's sake?—Oh, no! This won't work! Who will accept this counterfeit money here?'

And Mumtaz comes back home every day with his head hanging low. I keep staring with a fixed eye on the old and decrepit woman sitting on the opposite terrace. She appears like a stone statue from a distance. This statue gets erected every morning and stares all day into the void of the sky with stony eyes. Mumtaz had said that a week back this statue had life. It used to breathe. It spoke, laughed. But they say that one day a star fell from the sky and dazzled its eyes. Its breathing stopped. The old woman thinks that that star was a piece of her heart. Her son. But a goon thought he was a Muslim. And worthy of a beheading.

Therefore, they sent the statue here. So that she can come to this Muslim locality to find her star. And she spends the days gazing at the sky. Looking for her star with her dim, lifeless and cold eyes.

Oh, what do I do, Mumtaz! You shouldn't discuss news of the riots. I no longer have the strength to listen to it. The discussion has a void and that void can only be filled by Achha. And you will find your Achha. You say that I give you hollow consolations. My friend, there is an incredible change in you. The storm inside you has died. You have become a particle of suffering. You do not retain belief in yourself, no control. You are sick of my emotional wranglings. You will drive me mad too. And I do not wish to go mad. Shall I leave? Should I go?

I went to Qateel's this evening.* There wasn't a line of worry on this romantic poet's forehead. His curly hair had a new sheen and glow. His face shone in waves of splendour. He told me that he had married his Hindu actress friend. The Maulvi sahib from the local mosque had married them for five rupees and had said that if any scoundrel still considered her a Hindu—despite her having recited the kalimah—and wanted to kill her, then Qateel should inform him and he will set them right. I said: 'Qateel, forget what the Maulvi sahib said; you have saved a life with five

---

*Qateel Shifai (1919–2001) was the pen name of the Urdu poet Muhammed Aurangzeb. Qateel published over twenty collections of verse and wrote over 2,500 film songs for Indian and Pakistani films.

rupees. For me, the experience of this happiness is enough. And yes, tell me, what is the source of this splendid glow on your face?'

'The consummation of romance,' said Qateel blowing smoke rings into the sky. He now needed a new house because the neighbours had told him that he could not live there with a Hindu girl or the goons would set it ablaze.

29 August

I could not sit still anymore. That statue will continue to search in the void for stars. But where will it find that fallen star now? I came out in a state of restlessness. This roving life still retained the same passivity and stillness. But, a new bustle had indeed been born here. This bustle too was tired and pitiful. A new camp for refugees had been opened at the Walton School. And a new commotion in life had arisen with it. People were coming and going. Lorries filled with dead bodies passed in front of my eyes. These bloodied bodies had been sent by Indians to Pakistanis as a gift. And there was a commotion in the life of the recipients. Their faces seemed to say: 'We shall send an even better and grander gift to our friends and relatives so that we don't lose face in the community.' A river of love had spurted out. How terrible was this love. It did not have the balance of dance and melody but was as if someone would grab you by the shoulders and shake you, and say, 'I'd stab you if you don't love me.'

I went ahead. I kept walking and trying to make myself fall in love again with my dear and beloved Lahore. These buildings belong to which city? Where have these roads been brought from? From where have these people entered? I feel like standing at the square and shouting loudly: 'Brothers! Animals! Barbarians! Leave my city and go and live in the jungles of your ancestors. Who allowed you to come here? Go back to where you came from. Go, because you have still not managed to become human.'

But I could not shout from the square. People were saying that not a single Hindu or Sikh could now live in Lahore. Why? But why? It felt as if my brain had been struck. Why? Why could I not live here? I—I who have wandered these streets, who have stamped these roads with the sketches of my songs? The gleam of my tears, the echoes of my guffaws, and the flowers of my smiles are hidden in the walls of the monuments of this city. Who can stop me from living here? No, no, I will not leave! Madmen! I understand the responsibilities of my new *state* better than you.* I have rehearsed a life of the mind here. I have filled my colours into the doors and hallways of this city. This is my city. Mine. What do you know what is one's city? Go and ask Jawahar and Jinnah. Have they ever felt the touch of the tiles of the roads of my city? Have their eyes ever

---

*'State' is used in English in the original.

struck the bends and corners of this square? Have they ever felt the joy of loving this city? If not, then they have no right to order me to leave from here.

I asked a tongawala standing at one corner of the Mall Road: 'Baba, would you go to the station?'

The tongawala was Muslim. But if he was Muslim, then why did he not stab me with a knife? No, he could not have been Muslim. I climbed on to the tonga in wonder and doubt. The tonga began to move towards the station. The same road, the same curves, the same corners, but there was no sign of any Hindus or Sikhs. Such a large people—where had they disappeared? It is said that four hundred thousand Hindus and Sikhs used to live here. Where did they go? And the tongawala told me with great respect and in complete confidence that those kaffirs had gone to the camps.

Station—Lahore's grand and magnificent station—is mute. As if someone has strangled its neck. Silent. Hushed and still. You couldn't have heard yourself in the noise of the thousands of people here. But this noise could not dispel the new and unique silence of the station. A new iron fence had been erected around the station. And the military had control of it. Some men were bringing the wounded from the platform. Filled with cries, groans and moans, the station seemed to have become a house of mourning. The relief camp was in place. And volunteers were piling the wounded and the dead into lorries to take them away.

I shook my head; as if I was shaking off the dust and grime. Then with great calm, and in a very casual everyday manner, moved towards the ticket-booking counter. An unusual clerk was posted there—a military-man. I asked him: 'A ticket to Multan, please!'

And the soldier kept staring at me with his eyes wide open in disbelief. 'All lines have been closed!' How assured he was of the veracity of his response.

I came back to the Mall Road. Coffee House was closed. China Lunch Home too. And the street in front led to Sant Nagar—where my house was. I don't know why, but I had a feeling of great unfamiliarity with the street. But then I braved my heart and went in its direction. The whole area was desolate. Not a creature in sight. I knocked on many doors despite knowing that all houses had been adorned with big locks. And apart from the lovelorn caws of the crows and the shrieks of hungry birds, I found nothing else. All of them had left. How merciless were these people? They had deserted their precious streets.

Yes, here used to be the paanwala's shop. Here was the hospital. Here an old woman used to spin yarn at her spinning wheel. Here, the old cobbler used to repair and clean worn-down shoes. They have all left. The taps in the streets were still bleeding streams of water, as if to ask me: 'Poet! Will our sparkling white, pure water go waste like this? Where have the thirsty of this country gone? The military officers posted at the corner were perhaps trying to support the desolation. Cows and buffaloes were ambling around as they chose. Their udders were filled with milk. But no one was around to hear the plaintive appeals of this silvery, sweet and beautiful milk. The very air had been orphaned. And who knew where Adam and Eve had gone?

I felt like roaring out a loud guffaw so that the roofs of these houses blow away and the streams of water flowing from the taps rise and go join the clouds. So that when I open my eyes a plaintive desert is in front of me, and I am there all alone. And in this desert I give birth to new creations and a new life. New fruits, villages, and…and…

But my guffaw stopped in my throat. Because when I opened my eyes I had reached the middle of the Hindu-Sikh Refugee Camp. Having left heaven these people had arrived in hell. And they were happy. That their religion had been saved. A din, a commotion, clamour. People were loading their baggage on to big lorries to take it away. The shadows of unease and distress spread in all directions.

'Where are you going, friends? Descendants of rishis and munis, where are you going?'

Everyone had vague smiles of victory on their lips. 'We are going to India, our country, our nation—'

And I left the camp of my countrymen and came to the foreign country. Mumtaz had still not come.

Perhaps he has still not been able to free his love from the jungle of the Pathans' lorries.

31 August

I met Arif today after about twenty days. His eyes seemed to sparkle the moment he saw me. I found this spark very endearing. As if I was looking into a mirror. And I felt as if I had been sifting through ashes looking for it for centuries. 'Arif! Where had you hidden such devotion all along? Let me bathe in this sea of light to my heart's content!'

During our conversation, a shadow seemed to rise from behind the sparkle in his eyes. This was the shadow of grief. I could recognize this shadow immediately. Because these days, it is not life but shadows that must be addressed. Arif told me that he was now going to the camp which his family had managed to reach after undergoing much struggle, having been pillaged on their way from Amritsar. A young sister is not to be found. The father insists on living in Amritsar. And Arif is worried. This worry has a little pleasure, some bitterness, and some sadness. At the father's stubbornness, there is a wave of joy rising in Arif's eyes, but sadness is clouding it as he imagines the conclusion of this obstinacy. This is why he is filled with confusion.

'Fikr, comrade! Where were you? I was very worried about you! Come friend, take me to your bosom.' And as he started embracing me, I said, 'It is crucial for you to go visit your family at the camp now. I will come meet you tomorrow. Your father's insistence has also put me in confusion. But let's leave that for tomorrow. Tomorrow I will move here. I cannot live in Achhrah anymore. I do not find the spark there that I find in your eyes.'

And I kept wandering around with Qateel. And Qateel passed time by smoking away bidis. His film company had closed down due to losses. The proprietor had run away, and he was now hungry. Hunger had manifested itself in the form of the bidi. And he was on the lookout for a house, but unlike a month ago there was no dearth of houses in Lahore anymore. Because the occupants of houses had fled, leaving the houses vacant for us. And they were inviting us after every few steps. Walking around, we soon found a grand empty building in Paisa Akhbar which used to belong to a Hindu trader.* We occupied it. Qateel did, Arif did, I did.

Tomorrow morning all of us would move into this magnificent building. This house lies in an area which

---

*Paisa Akhbar Street in Lahore exists till date. *Paisa Akhbar* (Penny Newspaper) was a popular Urdu newspaper published in Lahore, British India. It was established in 1887 by Maulana Muhammad Hussain Azad and Nisar Ali Shohrat. The daily published news stories and editorials aimed at a general readership and supported nationalistic causes.

is the base of the thugs. The brave goons from here had carried out exemplary acts during the riots. A thug from here had promised a widow and her two young sons his protection. Had taken five thousand rupees from the widow for this brave act. And then to fulfill his promise had thrown them into the house on fire next door. And for this great act, the leader of the locality had granted him permission to set fire to three more houses so that he could lead a life of probity.

I am leaving Achhrah tomorrow. Mumtaz's face has disappeared from my eyes. His Platonic pride is caught in a whirl. He takes cold showers five times a day. Smokes the hukkah a lot. He is hiding something from me and the way he is hiding it is not beyond my ken. A calamity of anxiety has fallen on him, and he does not want to acknowledge it. And I am thinking, I wish, I could share the burden of this catastrophe with him. But to share with this strange person in his troubles is no child's play. He presents the darkest facets of everything I say. And then it feels as if he is telling me not to think anymore, nor say anything else. He does not wish to be deluded, although he is not unfamiliar with the bliss of delusions. But I have failed to give him that bliss. And my bones seem to be falling apart once again. My veins are again taut. I will have to disappear from Mumtaz's sight for some time.

I have been thinking all day about an arresting piece of news. The Maharaja of Patiala Estate has announced that a large section of his army has reneged, and deserted along with a big part of his arsenal. The Maharaja is said to feel immense regret at this event. But, really, what was in his control? When an army reneges it does not do so at the suggestion of the maharaja. But what I can still not understand is where did this traitorous army go? Till the time that this is not properly investigated, what conjectures may be made! Neither is there any need for such guesswork. Maharaja Sahib can never commit such a common, unroyal act and instigate his forces to join the thugs in murder and loot.

Tomorrow, if the forces of the nawabs and rajas of Kashmir, Bhopal, Bahawallpur, Hyderabad and Faridkot too turn coat then what will become of the state machinery of these estates? After all, in India and Pakistan there aren't one or two, but three hundred and sixty royal estates. And they haven't attained independence yet. Despite the departure of the English they are still complying by old norms and traditions, and are sovereign unto themselves. And the forces there can rebel, carrying away the arms in the arsenals.

One country has three hundred and sixty plus two—three hundred and sixty two—rulers. Oh my, Allah! What will become of it?

What Place Is This?

(Ye Kaunsa Maqaam Hai)

2 September

Why is this happening?
 Why is *this* happening?
 Why *is* this happening?*

I sit waiting expectantly with the hem of my kurta spread out, pleading for light. But in the terrible and strong blasts of darkness my kurta flaps around. I can hear the sounds of this flapping quite clearly. Kapoor was right. We, the representatives of knowledge, civilization, culture, literature and science, are deluding ourselves. The estimates of the people and the illiterate sections turn out to be more accurate than ours. And I am thinking, was Kapoor really right? Are we really ignorant? Why can't we hear the pulse of the people? Why don't people come true on our expectations and tests? I say, this cannot be, that people who have lived together for centuries can reduce to ashes each other's huts, houses and fields and then burst out into loud guffaws. And can force each other to break with traditions of centuries just to raise slogans in praise and approval.

---

*Translator's emphases.

The fire is spreading. The darkness grows. And a bloody river of hatred, contempt and destruction has risen and roars into all the towns and villages of the Punjab. And both parts of the Punjab have become the battlefields of Cain and Abel. Don't your eyes weep those tears? Does your heart not experience that agitation?...which are felt upon separating one brother from another.

Have the emotions associated with parting, separation and longing become quiescent or callous? Oh, how do you bear that the guffaw of Mohammed Hasan from the corner of the street has stopped forever. From another doorstep, the humming of Ram Parshad is heard no more. Who told you that this guffaw was not ours? That humming was alien? And then who do you call, standing upon the corpses of these strange guffaws and that alien humming? Who are you welcoming? Who do you look to? Your hope-filled eyes wait for whom? Who is this who comes wearing a saffron dress and crying for Shivaji and Ramarajya?* Or the one in the green uniform that shines with the crescent moon and star? You have even begun to recognize him. What is he saying to you? That you should strangle the throat of this guffaw? Take a knife to this humming?—and then, and then—you

---

*Shivaji: Maratha ruler who fought against last great Mughal Emperor, Aurangzeb (d. 1707).

are hypnotized, your eyes are closing. Your lips are stitched together. And you move forward like animals and beasts. You have shot your Mohammed Hasan, your Ram Parshad and your Ram Singh. And then long spears have marched ahead. Guns have raised their heads. Machine guns have found their rickety ways in. And then from the rear the rebel Ayodhyapati and Caliphate forces join as your reinforcements.* So that your morale may never drop. The fight for jihad and dharmayuddha does not die. A clamour has arisen. Children are screaming. Mothers are worrying. And wives have been separated from their husbands. Girls have lost their honour. Tears dry up before they fall. And beauty has died and love has lost its madness, and you...and you...and you?

What about you? So you are incapacitated. Blind. A beggar. In the hem of your shirt, in your begging bowl, lies a piece of alms which you are throwing up in the open air again and again and staining it with blood. This piece is getting coloured. It is gaining in splendour heated by the flames of fires. And you can't contain yourself with the attainment of such happiness. You are creating piles of corpses. You think your mendicancy is gaining in stature by conquering the timid glances of maidens, putting flower-like children on the spike, making Mohammed Hasan feel

---

*Ayodhyapati: Ram, as the ruler of Ayodhya.

a sense of alienation, and pointing the gun at Ram Parshad? And that you are stepping towards the acme of humanity? Malechhas clear our village. Kaffir! Leave our neighbourhood. Guffaws, run for your lives! Humming, run posthaste from here. We have got our long-lost heaven. We have our…

And I asked Arif: 'Have you found your cousin? Your mother's sister's daughter? But perhaps even Arif was living in a dream. And now the dream sequences have broken. As if something has come and fallen in the middle with a thud—perhaps, Ramarajya? And like me, he is also looking for the middle link to try to join the dreams.

'And then?' He tried to give his head a jerk as if trying to remember something. 'And then the sailors went on strike and the Bengali farmers wore handcuffs, when 1946 raised its angry and bold eyelids, when Azad Hind Fauj made each and every village echo with the cries of "Dilli Chalo…then…then…"'*

'Then…what happened after this, Comrade Fikr?'—'Then a tempest arrived, black, yellow, blue—can't quite remember the true colour of it—and trees were uprooted. It was a strange storm. Completely different from the usual ones. It was going in the opposite direction. And strikes, handcuffs, they all

---

*Azad Hind Fauj was the army put together by Subhash Chandra Bose with the help of Japan to fight against the British for Indian freedom.

disappeared in it, and with the terrible howling of the gale, one couldn't hear another sound. It felt as if it wasn't a storm at all, it was a fabricated whirlwind. As it rose and fell, its squalls and winds were sweeping everything with it. And their touch left a weird, artificial happiness in the heart. Some people said this was the touch of freedom. Then why were bagpipes playing in Buckingham Palace? Why were mills, factories and estates dancing with joy? Why was the song of my happiness rising from their lips? What kind of a storm was this? This was the middle link. And I said to Arif, shaking him up: 'Now you don't try to connect the dream. This song of happiness has reached Delhi. And those dressed in saffron robes are playing Holi with blood there too. Buckingham Palace and Shivaji have signed a pact. Come, let's go to the office.'

I have decided to properly start going to office from today. Signs of normality are starting to appear in Lahore. And I am trying to forget a lot by hiding behind this normality. I am getting busy in the desire to find a routine to life again. I have grown used to hearing everything. The arrow has now left the bow. But I am still trying my best to get past the scary thought that someone may try to cause harm to the Jama Masjid in Delhi. Jamia Millia's intelligent students are going to the school. There is a delicate chill in the shade of the Qutub Minar, and I am going to office! Escapist that I am! Representative of Progressive writing! Long live escapist writing!

5 *September*

Everyone was shocked. But everyone was silent. I was neither shocked nor silent. I was busy creating my routine. I had grown used to hearing everything: today, in such and such a town, so many Hindu-Sikhs had been gunned down; at that station 2,000 Muslims were put under the sword; today, in such-and-such district young women were denuded and paraded naked on the streets of free India; a train arrived empty today except for only two injured people, it had lightened itself of the cargo of the corpses on the way. Only this much? Tell me some bigger news. Tell me that today there is not a single human left in the Punjab! Only a few people of the main ministries are left, whom death has left behind to govern. Tell me that Jawaharlal has been killed today in Connaught Place by goons beating him to death with sticks, because he had recklessly come out of his mansion barefoot, and had ordered for the looting and plundering goons to be shot. And in honour of the order of the prime minister of India, the bullets in the guns of the soldiers had gone numb. And Jawaharlal had stepped forward for his white cap to be made the new target. Tell me that...that...but what use will that be? I have grown used to hearing all this.

WHAT PLACE IS THIS?

Today, Qateel berated Arif a lot. Because he has handed over to the police all the goods from the house he has occupied. He should have kept some of the stuff for himself too. Some chair, some radio set, some sofa. Oi, idiot! All your belongings were looted in Amritsar. Your house was burnt down. And you go around holding your hollow honesty close to your chest. Arif was quiet. There was darkness in front of his eyes. And in this darkness, mobs of people with their gaping mouths were passing by. They were ransacking homes. They were looting homes in every village, every town of the Punjab. And mounds of silk dupattas, jewellery, beddings and corpses were gathered by the railway lines. And with their cavernous mouths, everyone in the mob was trying to satisfy their hunger. All bounds of hunger had been broken today. Today was the day for prosperity. The old law was breathing its last, and the new law was still being organized and arranged, and people were looting people. And books lay sprawled on the charpoy in front of me. Two slates, three-four notebooks, one tablet.* And this loot had belonged to one fifth-grader. Whose learning had been left incomplete. And who could not take his treasure trove of learning with him when he had to flee for his life. And all of it had been left on this charpoy. All of it lay in front of me: 'Ma, give me

---

*Wooden tablet for writing that a lot of students used at this time.

my slate, my books, my notebooks! Those were mine, Ma! I had even written my name on them! I used to read them every day. I write on them, daily. Ma, bring me those books, I don't want new ones. Bring me my books—Ma!—Ma!

But the child's cries got crushed in the increasing clamour that was rising from the lower floors of the house. This was the noise of new, new beggars, refugees, who were asking for roti. The grand Chowdhury* of the neighbourhood had started a free food service. And roti, daal and rice were being distributed. The refugees were giving him their blessings. How good is the Chowdhury. God will reward him for this.

And I told Qateel's wife that God has already rewarded this Chowdhury. He has occupied four houses. See, how good he is, the poor guy! They say he is a millionaire anyway. He prays five times a day too. And occupies houses. And distributes rice. And gathers blessings. And—Qateel, Arif and I finally met today at Nizam Hotel for tea after the hiatus. And went on debating literature and science. And Anarkali went on getting louder with its din. The noise had the manner of Ghalib's and Mir's ghazals. This made me feel as if Anarkali were a bazaar in Egypt where a lovely Japanese doll had landed—Arey, Arif! What

---

*Term employed for landlords or local big men, is also a caste name that indicates Brahmins in different part of India, although many can be Muslim too.

has happened? Arif told me that a caravan had just arrived from Delhi. The Indian capital was painted poppy-red. And the city 'where dwelt only the chosen from every walk of life',* is now filled with men in saffron robes, deserter armies and missing arsenals to set those people right. They have entered like victors, and Nadir Shah's soldiers have started the bloodbath of Delhi.

'Can you tell me who swore at Nadir Shah?'**

'Yes, I can tell. That insult—that taunt—that's right, Nadir Shah is a victor! And Mir's and Ghalib's ways had become slavish. And slaves have no call to live in an independent country. And the caravan of Muslims from Delhi has reached Lahore, and Jawaharlal is begging, holding out the hems of his shirt in supplication. Begging for peace, begging for civilization. And Gandhi's soul has been shaken, and he has run from Calcutta, gathering his dhoti and stick. 'Hear, hear! The Mussulman is our brother!

---

*'*Rehte thay muntakhab hi jahaan rozgaar ke*'—is a popular verse of unknown provenance commonly attributed to Mir Taqi Mir. Refer to *Beloved Delhi: A Mughal City and Her Greatest Poets*, Saif Mahmood (Speaking Tiger, 2018) for the complete poem and translation.

**Nadir Shah, the Persian king's soldiers ransacked Delhi in 1739, killing over half of its population. He is supposed to have given the order to slaughter Delhi because of an insult to himself or to his soldiers, and possibly the death of some soldiers at the hands of civilian shopkeepers.

Why do you kill him? If you kill him then kill me too!'—Hunh, the idiot! How will it help us if they kill you? Don't come. Let your prayer meetings remain where they are. Take your fasts and your bhajans and go to some peak in the Himalayas. What use are you here? Why do you get in the middle of our fight, between us brothers? What right do you have? You are the one who destroyed us! Did not allow us to remain worth a cowrie!

But Gandhi is still trapped in the lie of the sincerity of his stupidity. And he has come to Delhi. And he stands leaning his stick against the steps of the Jama Masjid. Come, come! I will recite the verses of the Qur'an to you. You Veda junkies, worshippers of Krishna, descendants of Nanak's, come sing with me in this desert melody and air, this Arabic tune, come sing with me. Sing, sing! O People—sing!

But Gandhi is singing alone. And Arif and Qateel and I are drinking our tea. And my Ghalib's tones are ascendant in Anarkali. And a caravan from Lyallpur is going to India on foot.* A mob of howling men has descended on the caravan causing a stampede. And the noise of the stampede has echoed into Gandhi's ears. And Gandhi is shouting: 'Kill me too! Kill me too! Kill Gandhi too!'

---

*Lyallpur: Named after its founder Sir James Broadwood Lyall in 1892, is a city in Punjab, renamed as Faisalabad in Pakistan in 1979.

8 September

There was a king in the bygone era called Muhammad Tughlaq, whose job was to move his subjects from one city to another and to rule them.* Today, my mind is on the India of 400 years ago. Muhammad Tughlaq is travelling with his subjects and thousands are dying every day because of hunger, disease and fatigue. Their lips are dry, no sign of water anywhere. But the king called Muhammad Tughlaq is fulfilling his ambition. He is the king, deputy of God.

And after 400 years when the populace has still not been able to rid itself of the yoke of kingship, it is dying yet again because of hunger, travel and fatigue. On both sides, the kings are carrying their subjects around. The transfer of nine million people has been accepted. Nine million people are living in camps, leaving their ploughs and farms, their bullocks and their homes. I wonder if doing this was necessary. Many statesmen think that doing this was not only necessary but also natural. Why should anyone live as a slave in another's country? I am a fool. Arif's father,

---

*Muhammad Bin Tughlaq: Sultan of Delhi from 1325 to 1351. He moved his capital from Delhi to Daulatabad in the Deccan, in 1327 as he believed a more centrally located capital would benefit his empire. He then moved it back to Delhi in 1335 as he felt the transfer had been a failure. Both migrations of the court and the people of the capital city led to widespread misery.

who considers Amritsar his native land and is not ready to step out of his house, is a fool.

What will happen now? Where are we going? What kind of rulers are these? What sort of subjects are these? What is this freedom? I am surrounded by innumerable questions yet again. A frightful storm of devastation and destruction rises from the border at Wagah. Hatred has assumed the shape of truth. People are crossing this line from here to there and from there to here by dying, running, getting their legs chopped off, having their heads smashed, losing their children, having their honour violated, shouting and screaming. On one side of the line, the tricolour flies, and a crowd shouts the slogan: 'Hindustan zindabad.' On the other side, the crescent flag flies, and the people gleefully shout out: 'Pakistan zindabad.' Man has created a curious game of life and death for man. A tamasha is being played out. There is death on one side of the line and life on the other—this side is death and that side is life. Is this line the standard of life and the touchstone of death?

Yes! This is the line, and this line is immutable. And we have drawn it, what will you do to us? We are your king, alias Muhammad Tughlaq. You are only the people, alias the base. Shout slogans. Shout slogans even more loudly. What can we do? We are also helpless. You had made our life impossible. You fight, drink each other's blood, burn down each other's homes to ashes, for whom?—Only for us. And we are also fully aware of our responsibility. We respect your emotions. And we have accepted the transfer of populations. And had we not accepted this, then not one of you would have survived. We did this because it was necessary for peace. We have no blame in this. We did not ask you to commit this bloodbath. You just wanted a government and we have gotten it due to our good fortune. If you insist on fighting even now, keep looking at each other with eyes full of hatred, then it will be better for each of you that you leave your homes, your houses, extinguish your beauty, strangle your loves, and come, crossing the line. Come! Idiots! Animals! Barbarians! Brothers! Come here! Let us govern in peace. And Sahir Ludhianvi* is wailing and heaving with sobs, from Delhi, where he is reading the elegy for the Punjab:

> Friends! For years, I wove dreams
> of the stars and the moon, for you,
> but today on my torn shirt,
> there is nothing but the dirt of the road.

---

*Sahir Ludhianvi (1921–80) was the pen name of major Urdu poet and Hindi-film lyricist, Abdul Hayee. Born in Ludhiana, Sahir settled in Lahore in 1943. However, after Partition he fled to Bombay in 1949, unable to live in Pakistan. He was a hugely popular and critically acclaimed writer. Sahir won two Filmfares for his songs, and the Padma Shri Award given by the Indian state.

> My songs have choked in my harp,
> all notes lie buried in the mound of screams.
> Give me the alms of peace and civilization,
> the melody of my songs, my notes, my flute,
> hand them to my wounded lips, again.

But who listens to Sahir's cries and screams? How can the bard's broken flute be repaired? O Bard! All of us are beggars today, but no one drops any alms in our bowls. Who has the strength to listen to your songs today? Who need recognize the face of your pain, grief and protest? You may go on screaming, Gandhi kept beseeching, I may keep crying, Arif may howl—but you know these cries go, bang themselves against the Wagah border and are reduced to smithereens. Sahir, what does it matter if our Punjab is lost, but the border at Wagah has come into being! The forces of rajas and maharajas revolted. At least, the religion of Hindus and Muslims has been saved. Temples and mosques have been saved from desecrations. And haven't you heard that not a single namazi is left east of the Wagah border? And there is gambling in mosques and the Noble Qur'an lies in the drains. And that not a single pujari is left west of Wagah. Mandirs and gurudwaras lie in desolation. The idols of gods lie with the rubbish. Is this not enough? And here you are the people's bard! Sending the echoes of your screams on the airwaves to gain all this back? That your lost tune, your broken flute be returned to you? In the heaven of fools, who listens to such a creature of hell as you, my friend?

Today Maulana Salahuddin was stunned to see me at the Paisa Akhbar square.* 'Arey, you! You, here? Come this way! To the corner over here!' And in a whispering manner filled with pity and commiseration, began to ask me: 'You? You, in this terrible neighbourhood?—Have you gone mad? Okay, okay! Are you, okay? This is incredible! What have you been doing? Don't stay here! You come to my place. That's a safer locality. But, no, no, why don't you go away? I will also go. I will go to Delhi. How can I live here?'

Maulana was very shaken. I spoke in a fully confident manner, 'Maulana, the heart does not wish to leave Lahore. But why are you going to Delhi? In Delhi there is...'

'Yes, yes. But how can I live here. My one house was burnt down. The goons have looted all the goods from my other house. What do I do? What is going on? What can I even do?'

Yes, what could Maulana do? If only Maulana

---

*Maulana Salahuddin Ahmed (1902–64) was the editor of the prestigious Urdu literary journal *Adabi Duniya*, and had published writers such as Krishen Chander and Rajinder Singh Bedi. He was associated with the Progressive Writer's Movement as well as the Modernist Halqa-i-arbab-i-Zauq, or the circle of the keepers of taste.

were also a thug. What did he get by being civilized? Only that he had his property plundered, and now is contemplating crossing the Wagah border?

10 September

Arguments are habitual with Arif. What a bad habit! But acute political acumen and astute philosophical health have made Arif's arguments and debates a favourite and dearly beloved of mine. He would often get lost and entangled in debates in these times of fear, frenzy and barbarity. Affected by the emotions of these days he often changes, if not prevaricates, the direction of the debates. But I try to support him. I don't know why, but he seems affected by my personality. I hope he doesn't end up losing out by agreeing with me. Because, these days, I have gotten very emotional. For how could the point of view for which we worked for fifteen years, all that we wrote, all that we thought, how could it all be laid waste so easily at the hands of political mismanagement? What had we done? Is this why we fought the British? So we could be confronted by the wrongful murders of thousands of humans? Should we also change our worldview? Should we lose our faith in humans? What are we to gain? What is the use? Everything is useless, Arif miyan. We ought to die now. So that we do not continue to be misguided by the charming lie of humanity's better future.

And Arif got agitated upon hearing this. His penchant for argumentation came back to the fore, and then he took me through the nitty-gritty of his views on the praise of the people and the right of self-rule, and began to explain its specificities. I am indeed a fan of serious philosophical discussions, but my dear Arif! Have you thought about what is the status of religion for us now?

'Religion? Religion has fought its last war on the unfortunate territory of India. And it has been routed badly!' Arif was so full of hope.

'But my heart wants to write a poem where I can strangle my laughter, my hopes and any philosophical wisdom. And then go to a mosque and begin performing the duties of an Imam, or go to a temple to discharge the duties of a priest.

'This is escapism, and escapism is a deadly poison to our politics and literature.'

'But—but, the murder of emotions? Do you remember the soldier from yesterday, my dear Arif? Whom we met at Nagina Bakery?'

Arif's eyes became moist at the mention of the soldier. The soldier had loved and his love had been consummated in marriage. It had been only one and a half months since the wedding, and it was now in front of the soldier's eyes that some eight to ten Sikh goons carried his wife away. The soldier's head was reeling. His face had become the frozen statue of a cry.

He was immeasurably sad. Life for him had acquired the nature of a dried twig, and this strapping and burly soldier's eye would be tearful again and again. And…and…

'Oh, if I could, I would destroy those eyes. Arif, the present destruction's responsibility returns to these people. What do you say?'

Arif's eyes shone. I had seen this shine ten days back too. But now this shine had a venom and a fury. I got scared and he spoke agitatedly:

'Fikr, my brother! You are becoming a non-Marxist by cursing this people. By expressing hatred towards this people you show that even you have developed the poison of partisanship. Are you saying this to please the Muslims?'

Despite the strength of my affection for him, I was amazed at the existential accusations made by Arif. And he went on speaking: 'We cannot brand a whole people as murderers because of the mistakes of the leadership. If we do this then the real perpetrator will disappear from our eyes. Just as is happening in our present political times: flowing with the waves of partisanship we are drinking each other's blood, while the real culprits sit pretty in bungalows, estates, mansions and the Buckingham Palace, and we do not even see them. Our culprit is not a Sikh, not a Hindu, not a Muslim, but the soul of strife is imperial selfishness, which we do not see.'

Uff! How serious is this man! With what dispassionate clarity he speaks! But I feel that the love of the soldier's moist eye cannot bear with this seriousness. Isn't his culprit that Sikh, who destroyed the garden of his love? Then, who is the real culprit? How can I explain to the soldier that his real culprit is hidden in some bungalow?

Thirteen hundred people died of cholera at Walton Camp today. Thirteen hundred people who were born so that they could participate in the brilliant ordering, arrangement and completion of this world. Because those who rule over the ordering of this world brought them to the camp and killed them with cholera. So that the stupidity of this creation of a new world could be brought to fruition better and with greater beauty. This cholera, what is its religion? Doctor! Please give me the injection for the cholera of religion. And the doctored stared at me with his eyes wide open as he thought me mad.

I feel like seeing Walton Camp. So that I can see people dying. So that I can see them extend their hands to beg. Roasted gram is being distributed. Thousands of hands are folded. One old man clad in white has filled his hands with the gram, and has flung them into the air, towards the sky. And he has let out an immensely poisonous and terrible guffaw: 'Ha, ha, ha! Here, here, eat, eat to your heart's content. Here, gain blessings. Send ten sacks of gram to this dog's house!'

As if he was addressing God.

One young man distributing the gram has filled the hands of a young girl with it. And she is looking at him with grateful eyes. And the youth's lips are starting to quiver. And his eyes have a strange gleam, and I feel strong disgust. My mind is about to burst with the stink. How foul does man smell! Oh, the stink of the camp, the stink of man!

15 September

Today, when Qateel and Rahi returned empty-handed from Taunsa, instead of despondency, a new hope was born in my heart.* My in-laws were amazed: Qateel and Rahi were two Muslims, how could I expect Rani and Kailash** to be sent with them? Qateel told me that Khwaja was also amazed, wondering who is this person who cannot distinguish between Hindus and Muslims. What sort of a mind is this that believes that two Muslims would bring his Hindu wife safely back to him in these tensed communal times?

---

*Ahmad Rahi (1923–2002) was the pen name of Ghulam Ahmad, a Punjabi poet and writer from Pakistan, who was also active in the Indian Independence movement. Rahi worked for *Savera* magazine in Lahore. He wrote two books on the Partition riots, *Nim Nim Hawa* and *Tarinjan*. He used to meet with Sahir, Faiz and others at Pak Tea House in Lahore post-1947, where they carried on the Progressive Writers' group in Lahore.

**Rani was Fikr Taunsvi's second daughter and Kailash his wife.

I wonder about our times of social contradictions and absurdity. Crossing the treacherous distance of hundreds of miles, Qateel and Rahi reached Taunsa but returned empty handed. I was feeling very embarrassed in front of them. But Qateel told me that in Taunsa there is another foolish and embarrassed person like you, whose name is Khwaja Nizamuddin. He has taken the responsibility of the life and property of all Hindus of the district upon himself. He has declared that if a single Hindu were murdered in his region then he will put a terrible curse upon the Muslims. Khwaja is a great saint of our region.* Religion has thrown all of Punjab in the hell-fires of Nimrod. And religion has also taken thousands of Hindus under its benevolent shade. I have picked up the dictionary to find the true meaning of religion.

Qateel tells me that there was a ticket collector checking the roof of the train they were on, not for tickets but for Kaffirs. That man would be thrown off the moving train who hid infidelity in his dhoti or pajamas.** Scores of guffaws would follow, and the ticket collector would resume his checking in all sincerity. I wonder why Khwaja Nizamuddin was not a ticket collector. Why has he kept those Hindus close

---

*Pir does not have an exact approximation in English. Saint is used here.

**Uncircumcised men would be distinguished as non-Muslims or Kaffirs.

to his bosom? Why is he disrespecting religious law? Does he not know the meaning of religion? Does he think that the Hindus and Muslims who have lived together for centuries have lost their religious souls? And are they each other's companions in times of grief and pain and can't be separated from each other? Can they not be thrown off the top of trains? How foolish is this Khwaja? I salute his foolishness!

And here—thousands of miles away from this religious saint—I salute Gandhi who is still shouting from the stairs of the Jama Masjid that the Mussulman is our brother. Don't kill him. But the killings have not stopped yet. Delhi is once again poppy-red. And the saffron turbans look at Gandhi in amazement.

Today, Tufail Ahmed has arrived from Delhi with only the three pieces of clothes on his body. His newlywed wife is still trapped in a fearsome locality of Delhi. He had to climb out from the back wall of the Anjuman-i-Taraqqi-i-Urdu and hide in a thorny bush the whole day.* This master of politics and sociology,

---

*Anjuman-i-Taraqqi-i-Urdu is an organization for the promotion of Urdu with separate chapters in India (Anjuman-i-Taraqqi-i-Urdu Hind) and Pakistan (Anjuman-i-Taraqqi-i-Urdu Pakistan). It began in colonial India as Shoba-i-Taraqqi-i-Urdu as a part of the All India Muslim Educational Conference started by Sir Syed Ahmed. It championed a call for Pakistan and became responsible for the communalization of Urdu as a Muslim language, while the Nagari Pracharini Sabha effected the Hinduization of Hindi. Both contributed to the schism between Hindi and Urdu.

this thin little artist, litterateur, ran away with his life. He told us that the same Hindu boys who yesterday had decorated the gates of the Anjuman-i-Taraqqi-Urdu like a colourful bride, had turned to it today with petrol and matchsticks, and bloodthirsty pellets, to ravage it. Why did this change of minds happen? It is being said that the Hindus and Sikhs that went from the Punjab woke up the daydreaming, nincompoop denizens of Delhi. And waking up from their neglect, they ravaged the bride. Books were burnt. Invaluable first prints and manuscripts from the arts, literature and science were thrown to the flames. Because Urdu was the language of Muslims. Part of Islamic culture. Had travelled from Arabia and Iraq.* Hence, the social service of wiping out the very name and existence of this language had been undertaken. This symbol of Islamic culture had been destroyed. This symbol—in which the learned-in-Islam Premchand wrote,** in which the preacher of the Quran, Krishan Chander wrote,† in which Ratan Nath Sarshar of Arabian

---

*The author retains his sarcasm here, much as elsewhere. Urdu was in fact born and developed in India mainly in the Deccan (Hyderabad and elsewhere), and the north-Indian plains (Delhi, Lucknow and neighbouring areas).

**Premchand, one of the greatest writers of 20th-century Urdu-Hindi prose, was from a Kayastha Hindu background.

†Krishan Chander: Commonly acknowledged as another great prose artist in Urdu, author of *Gaddar* and *Mitti ke Sanam*, was also from a Hindu background.

descent wrote*—was burnt away as an offering for the protection of Hindu culture.

Mumtaz has been reunited with his Achha. And he is content. He saw countless corpses of Muslims lying by the 60-mile-long road on his way from Batala. He thinks Hindus and Sikhs have killed these Muslims. I also think so. Arif also thinks so. And he has been explaining the whole day to a clerk in our office that both Arif and I are wrong to only think so, as it is a given that Hindus and Sikhs killed those Muslims.

20 September

Today Arif and I went to the station. There was a vast swarm of dead, and almost senseless and lifeless, people that had gathered inside and outside the station, resting their heads on their dirty and matted sacks, pouches and beddings, stretched out in helplessness. They were the refugees. And had come from India. Their welcome had been accorded by disease, cholera, hunger and filth. Their eyes appeared like blocks of ice. Downcast and dejected faces, as if life had moved forward abandoning them. Their past had been stolen from them. The present was filled with filth and melancholy. The future was foggy. Travellers, where do you want to go? And their dry and dead lips

---

*Ratan Nath Dhar Sarshar (1846–1903), Urdu novelist and editor of *Awadh Akhbar*, was also a Hindu, probably of Kashmiri descent.

seemed to murmur: we want to die. Would you have a pill of poison?

A fifteen- or sixteen-year-old girl, with a deathly pallor on her face and lifeless legs, barely got up, took two steps, and undid her salwar to squat and pass water in front of hundreds of furtive eyes. And it was as if something flashed out and then went dark in my mind. What was this that broke in my head, Arif?

This was the sense of honour. Which was dying. This was the absorbent nature of maidenhood. Which had reached the centre of the traveller's inn to turn more like rice water. This youth, this beauty, this apathy? 'Uff! Come, Arif, let's go.' How quickly the standards of morals and polite behaviour were changing. We were shaping a new historical destination for progress and culture. On arriving at this destination a young girl loses her sense of propriety. The spirituality of the East breathes its last. Gita, the Quran, the Vedas, the Shariat, and law, all die here. This destination? Come, Arif! Let's go back. Centuries back. Let's go hide in caves. Let's get buried in the ground, let's dissolve in the air. We do not wish to head towards evolution. Let's go back.

27 September

We were all troubled. All thinking. Hoping that something would happen, something must give way— the thought was in everyone's head. Where have we reached?

Come. Come, let's weep over our deaths. Let's write elegies to the death of civilization. Abdullah Malik was exhausted.* Tufail, the playful and mischievous Tufail, had turned into a statue. Kalimullah was sad. Bari's eyes were moist and sad. And we were thinking—something must happen!

Later, we all gathered at Mumtaz's house. Dark and thick clouds of sadness had gathered over the Progressive writers of India and Pakistan. Even before the morning light could spread it had gotten caught in terrible darkness. The expansive and green garden of the Punjab had been destroyed in front of their artistic eyes. Flowers were crushed. Leaves had blown away. Nothing but blood and bodies could be seen on the roads. And shady trees had been battered out of shape by cannons and guns.

Peace, peace, peace!

The creators of literature and art wanted peace. 'We hate barbarity and the Changezian.'** They were saying that even in this atmosphere of hatred, when

---

*Abdullah Malik (1920–2003) was a journalist, historian and political writer, who remained committed to socialism and wished to see Pakistan emerge as a socialist state.

**Changez Khan or Genghis Khan (1162–1267), brutal conqueror, was the founder of the largest contiguous empire in the world. 'Changeziat' or the Changezian may be understood as a condemnation of brutal conquest, imperialism, or empire- or nation-making.

unceasing and tall waves of helplessness were being created, they still wished to arrest these waves or at least do something about them. This is why they had gathered in Mumtaz's house, and were trying to come to a decision.

They decided that to forge a holistic programme; a general meeting of all the writers should be called for the day after. I felt encouraged. The heralds of the future were lighting lamps in my gloom and pessimism. And I was coming alive again. Sahir had just returned to Lahore after spending two weeks in the bloody hullabaloo of Delhi. And in his special and unique manner, he was narrating the dastan of Delhi. What an invigorating life his stories had. The romantic and colourful* writer was recounting how he had lived in the house of a Sikh comrade. He told of how he would go to the radio station and other places with the Sikh comrade's wife. In times of terror and tragedy, how he kept wandering around, bearing his songs. He was saying that on the day of Independence he was in Bombay. And despite consciously trying his hardest to feel some happiness, he could not join in the celebrations. But once he came to Delhi it was as if someone had jangled the sitar of his heart with a fiddle. Blood and fire shocked his harp. And he wrote

---

*Raseela is used in the original, which can mean many things besides being colourful, full of the joie de vivre, artistic, interesting, etcetera.

the poem, 'Friends! For years, I wove dreams / of the stars and the moon, for you…'

And Mumtaz was saying, 'Oh, what a wonderful poem! Full of emotions and sincerity. Quite completely anti-Progressive…'

All writers were stunned. Waiting to ask why Mumtaz had not liked the poem.

All litterateurs came out of the meeting on to the street, and were astonished to find it pitch dark. Mumtaz's thoughts seemed to be correct. The government of East Punjab must have shut down the electricity. The whole city was drowned in absolute darkness. Soon the writers found the Mall Road flooded to their knees. A strange unease reigned. They were saying that the Sikhs had demolished the big dam on the river. And had stopped the power supply. Tonight there was to be no end to the destruction of Lahore.

One sahib went so far as to say that a large group of Sikhs was going to attack Lahore tonight. Uff! Restlessness and distress debilitated me again. 'What will happen now? Why are we headed towards the void of destruction and doom?' I couldn't sleep all night.

Flood, flood, flood!

The whole night Lahore remained restive with shouts and screams, and sounds of distress. The flood was rising every minute.

29 September

Neither was a dam demolished. Nor had the electricity been cut. No band of Sikhs ever attacked. Nature had taken its revenge against reactionary forces. Ravi and Sutlej had brimmed over, and a formidable flood had overrun middle Punjab. Many cities were drowning. Without caring in the least for blood and fire, without indulging or discriminating between Hindus and Muslims for their thirst for blood, razing refugee camps, tearing through railway lines and roads, and immersing entire settlements, water had run into the streets of cities. The biggest calamity had befallen the caravans migrating on foot, and the afflicted refugees. Progressive nature was teaching the murderous people a terrible lesson in equality. In the garbs of death, it had forced its way into the homes of Hindus, Sikhs and Muslims. And cities were being deserted. Houses were falling down. Crops were destroyed. And when the floods receded, the world saw that next to the rivers, thousands of empty carts and scattered goods lay motionless. The thousands of people who were to bring them into motion had been taken by the floods.

Today, Arif and I went to see the flood-affected areas of Lahore. Rarely has there been such a ghastly sight. Refugees had been camping here. The water had almost reached the roofs of houses. And people were screaming. Someone's son was lost. Somebody's wife could not be found. Someone else was wading through dirt to find his mother. And amidst this hubbub, the thugs' days were made. They were sweeping clean wealth worth thousands and lakhs of rupees. And hungry, naked and sick persons were standing on the road, weeping away their misery.

I could not see this sight for long, and we came back. We ran into Anjum on the way. Looking at his face made one feel as if an ocean of tears had dried up inside him, and could not escape through his eyes. And now a permanent state of depression had overtaken him. I could not gather the courage to ask him anything. Because I could no longer bear the smallest teardrop. But Arif did enquire. And what I feared, happened. I felt as if instead of Anjum I should start weeping bitterly with loud cries. But where was the ardour in my eyes? My tears would not even thaw. I had been deprived of the ability to cry for over two months now. I could not even properly express grief as a friend. And even lament no longer carried that effect, that truth, that emotion. This pain was the pain of the suicide of feeling and emotions. We all had strangled our throats. Anjum, Arif and I—all of us had done it.

In eastern Punjab, both of Anjum's sisters had been abducted and his old father had been shot dead!

For four–five days now I have experienced a strange, even bewildering, reality. It goes beyond the limits of amusement to providing glimpses of solemnity. Every day, our office manager prods me with friendly encouragements to convert to Islam. He prays five times a day and is a punctual, pious man with his fasts and prayers. Completely devoid of any political acumen or sense. A fan of religious ecstasy. Therefore, I felt sympathy with the honesty of his suggestions. But how can I take all this seriously?

I mentioned this to Mumtaz for sport. And began to laugh at the cultural contradictions of Punjabi Hindus and Muslims, at which Mumtaz counted off scores of differences with great solemnity. Anyway, why do I need to get so worked up about this insignificant little thing?

4 October

Whatever was meant to happen tomorrow, is happening today. It feels as if I am drawing near to some great calamity of my life. A tingling sensation seems to raise its hood and hiss around me. As if inviting me for a fight. I walk. I sit. I speak. I think. But that sensation does not leave me. Perhaps, I will have to call out someday and invite this reality in front of me. India has witnessed a major disaster already. History has turned a major tide. And here I seek my old, balanced life. I object to the fundamental movements of this tide. Which is why my heart is refusing to acknowledge the existence of this disaster, which is deciding the state of things on all sides. But...

Today, the manager repeated his suggestion again,

and said in a very responsible and conspiratorial tone that accepting it will be to my benefit. But the conception of gain that the manager has in his head, is not grasped by mine. I pity the poor manager. And in this pity, that sensation has also rustled in and raised its head again. Anyway, I see no cause for worry in this sequence of events.

Still, despite all this, I went on pondering over this mental shock the whole day. The one that had presented itself during the spat with Mumtaz. It was as if a man had broken a brightly glowing lightbulb by throwing a stone at it. And absolute darkness had prevailed all around. It was true that the bulb had not been broken contrary to my expectations, but it was the manner of it that was so greatly inartistic and common, which had immediately silenced me. I could not say a word. And I felt as if I had been mute for centuries. I did not lose my tongue at this stage for want of conversational ability. But I did fear the snapping of my mental chords. Therefore, I said to Mumtaz: 'Enough, Mumtaz! Forgive me now. I don't have the strength to go any further than this!'

Actually, the topic had started in a topsy-turvy manner! But I had been uttering all thoughts with extreme care, weighing each of them in my head well in advance. Mumtaz's claim was that if he were the dictator of Pakistan then he would not let a single Indian Muslim set foot in Pakistan. Even I was a fan of the goodwill, constructive nature and sincerity of this claim, but I had one doubt. Therefore, just to tease Mumtaz I added a rejoinder: 'But Pakistan was the collective call and movement of all Muslims of India. So after the victory of the campaign, all Muslims of the country have the right to claim its fruits. Not just a means to dictatorship—'

Mumtaz got riled up: 'I will install a metal fence at the Wagah border. And immediately prevent them from coming over. This is our country, not theirs.' And I tried to gently ask Mumtaz, 'What was the fault of the Indian Muslim in any of this? He has fought tooth and nail to realize Pakistan. And now if Hindu fascist fundamentalists are baiting him for his life over there, and here you are thinking of erecting the Great Wall of China at the Wagah border, then where should he go now? They are humans not animals, that they should be denied the fundamental rights of existence simply because they were born in India before the birth of Pakistan, despite having joined their voices with the call for the formation of Pakistan.'

'But we cannot allow every Muslim of the world to enter Pakistan! If tomorrow the Muslims of Iraq, Arabia and Kabul want to make Pakistan their country of residence, then will we grant them permission too?'

Mumtaz's logic was sound. But I felt as if something fundamental was slipping from under my feet. If fascist and regressive forces had not been in command of this movement then the results may have been different. And now that the results are still different, they grant all Indian Muslims the right to think of Pakistan as their homeland. I am happy to be a citizen of Pakistan myself. But it is different for me. If instead of me, the life of someone else is under threat, then how would their desire to save themselves allow faithful citizenship to triumph? This is also the state of the Muslims in India today, which is the same threat to life—to be murdered. This threat has a fascist root. And sitting in Lahore, Mumtaz could not grasp the effects of this threat. He wanted to erect a wall like the Great Wall of China. He had forgotten that the country of the Muslims of Iraq and Arabia is not Lahore. And moving beyond Amritsar these fascist waves had reached Delhi, Uttar Pradesh and Bombay. Mumtaz was looking at me with terribly glazed eyes. His rage had reached its limits. And keeping his composure with great difficulty he had said: 'Fikr sahib, please don't speak to me on this issue in future. I know that you speak to me as a Hindu. And I am a Muslim. I may get excited also. And the consequence of that excitement may be frightening!'

And then a huge lightbulb had crashed to the floor and broken into tiny little pieces. And I had grown silent. What an inartistic and common a sound the breaking of the bulb made!

The artist had cast a disgusting accusation at me: 'Hindu!'

Even if by calling himself 'Muslim', he had implicated himself too. But maybe he is proud of this accusation! I felt disgust at it. That sensation had reared its head again in front of me. And I was finding myself a centuries-old mute again.

Uff! Mumtaz thinks of me as a Hindu! If he wishes to think himself Muslim then I can have no strong or meaningful objection to it. But what right does he have to think of me as Hindu? He has hurt my pride. He has challenged my philosophical traditions, my intellectual training and my literary praxis. He has denied my iconoclastic* ego!

But I am quiet. I had had such an open and frank conversation with Mumtaz only because of the firm belief that he was a talented creator and artist, and artists are the representatives and record keepers of the fundamental truths of human life, and their humanism holds the place of religion for them, the secrets of space and time are revealed to them. Can the foundations of an artistic life be laid in the weak and alienating categories of Hindu/Muslim? My eyes started darting on the vast and innumerable pages of the literature and art of the past, and started turning them. Lightning sensations and goosebumps

---

*Kaffiraana in the original: literally idolatorous, but used here as unorthodox, rebellious, transgressive and therefore iconoclastic of the larger institutions, including organized religion.

pass through my body filled with restlessness and tension. Arif is looking at me as if to ask how this spark has been born in a cube of ice. And Mumtaz has gotten busy in speaking to another man. I can catch a few words like pistol, application, price and license. Maybe he was talking about buying a gun for self-defence, because he had told me over the past few days how essential it had become to purchase a gun for this purpose. My mind is rattled—as if sparks are glowing hot and cold in my head.

9 October

Attacks on the railcars have started again. The rebel and fugitive forces of the princely estates have still not returned to the captivity of their rajas and nawabs. Women and girls are still being abducted. The historical tradition of parading them is still being practiced. Gandhi's screams have brought a calm and the force of Delhi's rioting has lessened. And according to a leader, Gandhi is now threatening to come to Punjab to establish peace. And to preempt the danger of his arrival the intensity of attacks here has increased.

The Kashmir problem has reached its last stage today. One person was saying that the kingdom's Dogra forces have created a furore. The other thought the tribal clans of the North-West had carried out quick-fire attacks and plunder. And the Raja of Kashmir has declared his acceptance of the accession to the Indian

Union. And the politics of the world has been rattled. It is being said that the responsibility for the security of the Kashmiri people lies with the North-Western tribals. Someone says that the Indian Dominion will save the Kashmiri people. And the Kashmiri people are being ground between two millstones.

People—they have become indistinct dots. Aimless, whom no one sees. But whom everyone is claiming to see. The people are only being used to serve different aims and motives. What are the people? Only sheep! That powerful shepherds are shoving along their own paths. This wound of princely estates is the reminder of British imperialism. And to claim this wound, patients from both sides have attacked. And the puppeteers of London are watching the spectacle. And both sides are trapped in their strings. In the guise of slogans for the betterment of the people and by showing the magical vision of democracy, the farms and huts of hungry and naked Kashmiris are being burnt and destroyed. What is going on, Arif? Arif, my friend!

And Arif unites his voice with my soul's to say that even if Kashmir should be a part of Pakistan for geographical reasons, is accession the sole and fundamental question? Is the primary question not of the two fronts fast emerging in the political landscape of the world? Kashmir occupies an important position among those two fronts. The partition of India was also a demand of those fronts. Then…then…what will happen to the Kashmiri people? What about its chinars, its flowers, its springs, its cataracts and scenic views being prepared to be thrown in to the fires and storms of blood? Can they not be saved? Must the macabre dance of the puppeteer be played in this grand valley of beauty and romance? Arif, my friend, can you not cast a wider eye to look beyond? Come here. Look upon this vista, why are you stuck with India and Pakistan? Kashmir may join any dominion, the puppeteer's show will still go on. And then? And then?

Clouds of uncertainty and doubt have rolled again in front of me. And my mind, covered in the dust of grief and despair, is contemplating suicide. And Mumtaz is telling me: 'I deeply regret, Fikr bhai, that I got into that wrangle with you the other day. Actually, I shouldn't have started that debate. Actually... actually...please forgive me.' But I am caught in the wrangle of the puppeteer's horrifying play. I have left Mumtaz far behind. He is still caught in debates and meanings. And is explaining to the manager that the secret, and only, solution to the Kashmir problem is giving us arms with which we should attack Kashmir from the rear, since we have the rightful claim to Kashmir. And the manager is nodding his head at the revelation of this secret. He is swaying with agreement. And I am thinking that Mumtaz is my dear friend, and some waves of emotion have started running through my nerves. I am thinking of forgiving him.

And the manager is saying: 'Yes, Mumtaz sahib, till we don't get the arms how will we be able to provide protection? Haven't you heard what wonders arms and ammunition achieve? That poet sahib, whose collection of poems *Salsabil*,* has also been published, the one who lives in Misri Shah,** was putting the kaffirs to their doom, with a gun to his shoulder. He showed such bravado despite being a poet, Mumtaz sahib!'

And Arif thinks that the manager is definitely wrong. Such a hateful act cannot be expected of this poet.

15 October

Last night, I had my first exposure to the psychology of a fugitive.

I came to Sahir's home since last evening. And I am still confined here. Arif also stayed with me here last night. He didn't even go home. And he is trying to convince me that I shouldn't take any decision in a hurry. I should not leave Lahore like this. Sahir kept getting agitated. He had lost his cool in the same way yesterday too. And again today. He said: 'I will run away from here. I will go to Bombay.' And Arif in his loving and philosophical manner, arguing from

---

*Salsabil refers to a spring in heaven.

**Misri Shah is an extant neighbourhood in Lahore.

different positions, is trying to convince me to not go. Actually, he is trying to reduce his own nervous disarray and mental confusion. I was also arrested at this time by such nervous buzzing that I could not hear anything. I could only feel strongly that I am a fugitive, a runaway. I am a coward, who has come seeking asylum to Sahir's house. And tomorrow I might cross the Wagah border. And wish to turn around again and again to gaze at the streets, roads and bazaars of Lahore, and to be absorbed by them. But the sharp, shining point of the bullet is repeatedly telling me that if…if…

The manager had come and sat down next to me with immense secretiveness and sincerity. He was counselling Mumtaz: 'Mumtaz sahib! Please make Fikr sahib understand; a few thugs are after him. Please convince him to convert and become a Muslim. What difference does it make? To preserve life, after all, is key.'

And I don't know what Mumtaz had told him, but I had laughed aloud at it, as was my wont. Mumtaz had also attempted a laugh. And then, after laughing for a few minutes, he had left. And that vague sensation had again become active in my heart. And then after a few minutes some goons had come in. And had begun telling me to come out. And the two goons standing outside were pointing at me and whispering to each other. One of the goons who was inside was telling me to come out in the most domineering manner. The spring of reality and truth had burst forth from his quivering lips. And a noteworthy and brilliant memory of my life was being created along with it. I had asked the goon in an exceedingly gentle and pacifying manner: 'What do you wish to say to me?' And the goon had panicked. Even gotten a little scared. He was putting forward everything truthfully. And I had extended my hand to shake his. I was trying to put him at ease. He had jerked his hand back, probably trying to prevent it from getting contaminated. And I had recited the kalimah sharif to him. He had been left amazed. And had then plainly told me that they had learnt of my being Hindu, not just learnt of it, but that they were certain of it. Qateel and Rahi who were sitting next to me had quietly shaken their heads in disagreement. And the goon had challenged me with immense innocence and simplicity to come outside so that he could stab me to death. And I had asked him what his religion was? And the goon had said without any hesitation, 'I am a Muslim.' And I had asked him without hesitation, 'Have you read the Qur'an? Do you know how to offer namaz?' To which he had replied, 'I have no interest in such talk of yours. I haven't read the Qur'an, nor do I know namaz. But I am not a Hindu like you.' And I had expressed my disagreement with his views, 'I am a Muslim, because I have read the Qur'an and I know how to offer namaz.

Tell me, what else is needed to be a Muslim?' At this point, a trembling overtook the goon that was caused by his evident vexation.

And he had to accept my proposition that to go to the Big Mosque and get a testimonial from the Maulvi was the shariat's injunction! Qateel, Rahi and I had assured him that the testimonial will be shown to him tomorrow. And the thug had kept his hand on the knife in his pocket before accepting our proposition.

The manager had then gotten up from the office again to present me with his respectful and sincere whisper of a request. 'It is essential to satisfy these bastard thugs. How does it matter anyway?'—he was repeating as if by habit.

And Sahir had grown terribly excited in his heart and mind. 'What does it matter anyway?' He thundered at the manager in bewilderment. He threatened to get him and the goons arrested. And he got a threat in return for this: if he did not cease with his display of anger then he too would be stabbed to death.

And I was thinking—but what use is my thinking? The head of the law had been chopped off from its body. Jawaharlal and Jinnah had announced the founding of two new kinds of democracies. Democracy, which is the last stage of human progress. The very best arrangement for life. And I remember this verse by Iqbal:

People are counted in numbers, not weighed.*

And people were being counted and lined up. And those capable of being weighed and measured were being scared away by the blade of the knife. What does it matter if Jawaharlal was declaring the protection of minorities as the first call of duty of his democracy, and that as punishment for this malpractice he had to agree to the exchange of the populations? Or that Quaid-e-Azam was screaming himself hoarse calling the protection of the minority the elixir of immortality for his nation?** And that a member of his state was being given the undemocratic threat to convert? What does it matter?

And friends, what is religion? Some lines that run parallel to each other. Arey, how difficult is it to traverse the distance between these parallel lines? Kalimah, namaz and Qur'an. Sandhya, Veda and Bhagwan.† I can cross this intervening distance with more speed and beauty than you. Let alone the question of just crossing over, if you want, and wherever you want, I can stand on any of the lines any of you occupy and appear more handsome and attractive than any

---

*Original verse by Iqbal: '*bandoñ ko gina karte haiñ tola nahi karte*'.

**Quaid-e-Azam: The honorific title for M.A. Jinnah in Pakistan.

†Sandhya or Sandhyavandana: mandatory reciting of scriptural verses at morning, noon and evening, by the Dvija or the Brahmin Hindus who are considered twice-born through ritual.

among you. To fool you and to mesmerize you is as easy as to go buy paan with two paise. Tell me, should I buy you off like a two-paise paan? Qateel got a wife for five rupees, I can purchase religion for two paise.

But, O businessmen, first learn the manners of dealing in times of a crunch. *Narkh-i-baalaa kun ke arzaanii hunuuz.** Add some attraction, some art, a jangle to your ways of selling. I am an artist, I'd give my life for the melody of songs, the colour of paintings and the turn of a verse. You keep my soul as a pledge. But please throw the market goods into my lap with such force that I go away humming and swinging from your presence. But what is this?—What are you doing? You present your wares in such a vulgar manner that I feel ashamed to buy them.

And Arif went on convincing me the whole night. And my nervous jangling ebbed and flowed. Arif, if you tell me that I should convert to Islam, then I swear on God Almighty, on the Noble Qur'an, on the Prophet of Allah, that not only me, I would convert the whole world to Islam. But…but…Arif's lips were quivering. And he said, 'Fikr bhai, please do not pierce my heart anymore. Let me think of something, let me think of something.'

And he could not sleep at all that night. And went on thinking. Went on thinking.

---

*Persian phrase, literally meaning: 'Raise the price, while it is still expensive'—make hay while the sun shines.

Come, Let Us Look for the Dawn Again

(Aao Phir Subha ko Dhuundein)

17 October

Lahore has become twice as lively. It is laughing at the corpse of its old self; and with these guffaws it is giving birth to a new life. The historical gap that lay between the Hindu and Sikh emigration and the immigration of Muslim asylum seekers has been very quickly traversed. The cacophony of anarchy, fear, arson and stabbings seems to be subsiding. Lahore is now at peace. But the face of this peace matches neither autumn nor spring. There's remorse everywhere, and also the desire for creating a new life. But this creation is taking place in an extremely uncouth manner. People cross the Wagah border in the near-death stages of starvation. They wish to heave a sigh of relief in the heaven of Lahore. But Lahore's garden of heaven lies devastated. The leaves are scattered, the flowers have wilted. Thus, the refugees find no shelter. No respite is to be found. The waves of song rise in the heart only to die a quick death. With the ominous emotions of petulance, despair and death, the refugees have started ceaselessly roaming the streets of Lahore. Large, lonely and helpless groups dressed in old rags sit staring at the skies from under the trees on the footpaths. These people are conquerors, and have won the battle of faith against infidelity. They have entered Lahore to celebrate their victory. They have come running from Ambala, Rohtak, Jallandhar, Kapurthala, Panipat, Delhi and Saharanpur to celebrate their day of independence here. They have defeated the composite culture of Punjab with such aplomb in the battlefield that posterity will remember it.

It is a strange victory celebration that includes moans and cries. Complaints of the past are heard echoing around. The poor and famished segments are participating in this celebration by dragging their heels on the roads. Local and foreign goons are offering praise and approval, following up on their loot and plunder. Big men have captured big bungalows, so that in the celebratory gatherings of their soirees, no small or common man may be seated. The middle and honest classes start loitering on the streets when they cannot find another honest way of expressing their happiness. A film director has accepted the contract for starting a cycle stand in place of his cinema. A sixty-year-old man dressed in white is going around Anarkali Bazaar carrying the weight of his four young and single daughters on his delicate and weak eyelashes, and is looking for traders. A river of sympathy has risen among the local people. An internationally renowned artist—who, it is said, was fanning the flames of fire and blood during the riots—has come out to beg for old clothes and blankets for the refugees. A fat and old neophyte poet, who has earned the grace of both worlds by burning a godown full of films during the riots, has now arranged for a mushaira for the arrival of the refugees. Sahir has brought in the invitation and given it to me.

And Sahir's mother is saying: 'Fikr, my son, you should not leave the house. My dear, the times are really bad.' And these bad times have imprisoned the wanderer that is me. 'Ammi, this is my city. What danger can befall me here? Let me go, so that I can see how the new people have treated my city. How do they stroll in Lawrence Gardens?* Do they know the etiquette of taking a stroll on the Mall Road? Are they impressed by the magnificence and grandeur of the Anarkali, or not? Do they have the appetite to relish debate on art, philosophy and culture at China Lunch Home and the Coffee House? Sahir, I have heard that two Progressive ladies have arrived from India? Can I meet them?' 'No, my friend. Those Progressive ladies have donned the burqa since they got here. How can you meet them?' 'Right then, Ammi, I am going out to just see my city. I haven't committed any crime. I haven't murdered anyone. I haven't set fire to any

---

*Originally built as botanical gardens and modelled on Kew Gardens of London and named after John Lawrence, Viceroy of India from 1864 to 1869 the gardens were renamed as Bagh-e-Jinnah after the creation of Pakistan.

house. I haven't put a stop to the songs of the Punjab. I did not slit the throat of civilization with a knife.' And Ammi went on laughing at my simplicity, at my innocence. 'Come, son, have some tea. Sugar is not available. Have some with jaggery. Or would you like it with salt?' Sahir's eyes were growing moist as he was drafting a statement on the riots on behalf of the writers and artists of Pakistan.

Arif came thrice today to meet me. And Chaudhari too.* He is grieved that I had to face these incidents, and is trying to dissuade me from leaving. His face is anguish personified. He is perturbed. What, what is this that has happened? But he is getting rid of this worry by laughing with loud guffaws. These guffaws have glimpses of the same mental fortitude, and in these glimpses I am trying to draw the parallels of the future of man. Mumtaz kept trying to meet me but I could not meet him.

I have made the final decision to leave Lahore.

20 October

I am again caught in uncertainty. The desire to leave Lahore does not go from the hidden corners of my

---

*Chaudhry Barkat Ali was the founder of Maktaba-i-Urdu, a leading publishing house, and *Adab-i-Latif*, a leading Urdu journal. *Adab-i-Latif* published Saadat Hasan Manto's stories accused of obscenity, and the journal was also party to the court case.

soul. What torment, what agony this is. I wonder how pure is this stubbornness of mine that I stay on in Lahore to refute the conception and implementation of the transfer of populations. My obstinacy may carry individualistic tension, but there is a collective consciousness too that governs it. If a transfer of population had not been undertaken on this vast scale, then what danger would this have meant for Hinduism? What damage would this have caused Islam? And most importantly, how would this have harmed humanity?

Am I a foreigner now? Is Sahir a foreigner? Is Bari one? We spent the best moments of our life together, and as if in a trice, a wizard from Alif Laila has cast his great magic spell to tell us that we are now foreigners.* This is outlandish. The mind refuses to accept that at a distance of 20 miles begins a foreign nation, another alien culture. Can't there be a greater spell cast that will blow up this border to smithereens? A magical spell? The greatest word? And yesterday at the gathering of artists and writers, Sahir had

---

*Alif Laila: The original Arabic name of the Arabian Nights or the One Thousand and One Nights.

'The great magic spell': the original Urdu here uses ism-e-aazam or the greatest name, which is a name that is held to be greater than the ninety-nine names of Allah, and all powerful, and works as a master charm. It may also be understood to be the Biblical Word that was with God.

announced with great emotion: 'Come, all you artists and writers, let us band together into a new collective and forge ahead. From over there the Indian writers will come forward with the tricolour. We should both meet at the Wagah border, and exchange each other's flags. The Indian writers raising the crescent flag would march into Pakistan, and we would head into India waving the tricolour.'

This proposal had romance. It had passion. And upon hearing it, the faces of many writers began to glow with immodest joy. And many other writers had quietly thought in their heads of this proposal to be an object worthy of ridicule and mirth. One master poet who had suddenly turned communist after having been a loyal servant of the British for five years, was beating his chest loudly and shouting: 'We swear to bring humanity to life again through our pen, our art and our life.'

Malik's lips were trembling: 'We will go to every village and town to spread the message of peace, humanity and civilization.* We will enter the hearts of the people. We will call out to every man on the street, and tell them to learn to stay alive. Your lives are being slaughtered in the abattoirs of capitalists, rajas and nawabs. Come out of these abattoirs.'

A storm of love and passion had been triggered. It

---

*Abdullah Malik. Refer to note on page .

felt as if life was not dead yet. In this bloody wheel of time, there were still those alive and well who could light the lamps of the imagination of goodness and balance. And hatred and meanness have not yet strangled the throats of talent and song. What kind of people are these? Where are they from that they have managed to save themselves from showers of blood and whiplashes of fire?—Do you live in India? That India which is building its monument to religion and civilization on the kalimah and the Gayatri mantra? Where the foundations of politics are being laid in circumcisions? Have you never experienced the hatred of man against man, Punjabi against Punjabi, civilization versus civilization, and Allah against bhagwaan? What sort of people are you who rise to sing the raaga of love? Where are you looking? How does your sight rise to such heights, go so far, and plumb such depths?

The fogs of my mind are thinning away. I can see a little. Last night I had said to Arif: 'Arif, will we, a handful of writers, succeed in making amends for such a vast trauma? Would we be able to take the breadth of our vision and the echo of our emotions to the hateful and barbaric hearts of the people?' And Arif had interrupted me: 'By giving the label of hate and barbarity to the people, you are insulting the very foundations of revolution. My friend, the barbarians and fiends are not the people, but... We have crossed a crucial stage of history. Today, Empire's stratagem has worked. It has tried to take our people away from the real issues by hiding behind barbarity and brutality. And it has succeeded in these attempts. Now we have to start the journey of educating the minds of the masses' reaction against this practice. Come, friend, let us begin this journey. We have now reached a more difficult but more proper destination—'

And Arif went on talking. He was speaking like a man possessed, and I was listening like one. And in that moment I had forgotten everything: the goon, the knife, Muslims and my own fugitive status. What am I? Why do I get so worried at all these matters? These were all stages of my new journey—'Ammi, let me go, my comrades are waiting for me. Give me your aashirwad, Ammi, your son is embarking on a new journey.'

Sahir who has been running around all day getting signatures on his writers' declaration from different authors came to me and began saying: 'Fikr, did you hear Askari has refused to sign our declaration letter?[*] He refuses to recognize himself as a Pakistani writer! Fikr, comrade! I ask you why did he flee India to come to Pakistan? Why? But why?'

---

[*]Hasan Askari (1919–78): Born in Bulandshahr, United Provinces, British India, (now Uttar Pradesh, India), Askari was an Urdu scholar, critic and writer of note.

And Sahir's 'why' went on churning in my brain the whole night.

24 October

The pressure on Kashmir is increasing. Conditions worsen day by day. A new chapter of hatred has been opened. This hatred has been triggered immediately after the first, so that the continuum of hatred does not break. The blood of thousands of innocent Kashmiris is being spilt. Only because the British emperor had handed the fate of the people to the Maharaja when he was leaving, and the Maharaja's hand was in the hand of the Indian dominion. Thus, the foundations of the Indian dominion and that of Pakistan were laid in hatred. And this hatred had not yet heaved a sigh when this new hatred was tied up to the springs and gardens of Kashmir. Everything was clear. Our programme was fixed. The atmosphere was desperate. Passionate whirlwinds were flying on the streets and lanes of Lahore.

What will happen now?

Threats are being made here to march to Delhi, and from there to reach Peshawar. Minds are filled with worry again. A fog has gathered around too. Why don't these fogs clear away? Some fingers are seen dancing in it. Friends, recognize those dancing fingers!—Come, let me take your threat to my chest. Come, I will take you to Peshawar, and you to Delhi.

But, please, do acquire the etiquette to set foot in those cities prior to the march. I know that you retain unfortunate memories of Peshawar or Delhi in your hearts. But you also find a sense of familiarity in them. So, don't forget the familiarity now that you are going to your own; you are still giving threats like enemies and foreigners.

And on McLeod Road today, Sahir and I got into an argument with a Progressive litterateur and poet. It is said that he has occupied two–three houses these days so that thugs don't steal the precious goods in them. And he was loudly thundering to proclaim: 'We must capture Kashmir by any means, just or unjust.'

And I wondered if the Progressive writer thought only of capturing Kashmir as the solution to end the sorrows of the Kashmiris? Is he also not looking at the waves of international politics which are coming so thick and fast from opposing ends of the spectrum, only to submerge and overwhelm the reservoir?

Is conquest the only cure? Can the face of the cure not be changed?

Today, the Quaid-e-Azam delivered a lecture to a gathering of lakhs in Lahore. And the suddenly turned-Communist poet read a poem in his honour. All of Lahore had come out to listen to his speech, and Sahir and other comrades had heard it on the radio. And we had all balked at the poem of Firdausi Islam.

27 October

Comrade Parashar came to the party office yesterday. He had come from Amritsar. He was not too surprised to find me still in Lahore. And I was also not too happy to see him—why was I not happy? I should have jumped for joy at seeing him. I had seen a 'Hindu' face after a full two months. I had been starved of seeing a Hindu face. But what sort of a Hindu was Parashar? Coming to Lahore from Amritsar in these dangerous times, and debating boldly with the Muslim comrades at the party office on different political topics. I wanted that Hindu who had run away from Lahore in fright, and did not wish to come back to Lahore anymore. Parashar asked: 'Will you come to Amritsar?' I refused. Comrade Rahi said in jest: 'We desperately need minorities in Pakistan. And Comrade Fikr will fill this need of ours.' And I was left wondering how much seriousness was there in this jest, and what thick fogs covered this serious reality. And the faces of all Comrades sitting in the party office had grown solemn as if to say that we will tear through these thick fogs. We shall light a flame and invite the world to come bear witness in its light—come, identify the faces of your culprits.

But the culprits had worn royal crowns and disappeared in front of our eyes. They were busy occupying large houses, bungalows and factories. And the people were hungry, naked, dragging their feet through the dust on the streets. With their beddings spread underneath some tree or the other, they were waiting for the great magic charm. And the eyes of the comrades were expectant. A storm was dying down. But its footprints were still quivering and were looking at a new storm rising in the depths of their chests. The people did not want dharma or mazhab, not faith, neither the Vedas, nor the Shariat. They needed a society. They had hopes for food. They had the desire to live. And these they were unable to find. Fascism had burnt the crops away with its fires. But the sparks left underneath the layers of burnt crops were starting to catch fire again. They will become a full-fledged fire again, and from these red-red fires, a new crop will grow. And in that swaying red light, the faces of the culprits will be identified.

What does it matter if even after running around in the sun and dust for a month and a half, Sahir has still not been allotted a home? What does it matter if the sixteen-year-old girl from the station no longer retains a sense of shame or honour? If I don't experience the expected happiness at meeting Parashar? What if Maulana Salahuddin's house was looted? So what? Justice is not dead yet. There is still breath left in virtue. Happiness is not extinguished yet. Those farmers, who had come to the party office in the morning having rescued a Hindu family, and had asked for them to be delivered to the refugee camp, still breathe in this world.

Today I went with Sahir and Rahi to Paramount Hotel for tea. The hotel's dark-skinned, plump proprietor, who was wearing a Peshawari sandal, Punjabi salwar and Turkish topi was sitting in the manner of a special display. He would get up every second minute, go out, walk around, stroll about as if to showcase his existence. As if he wished to say to everyone: 'Look! Look, I also am! And I have realized a big secret.' I kept looking at him in wonder and amazement. Eventually, I asked Rahi, and he told me that till a month back this person was a Hindu and had newly converted to Islam. I found great mirth in this. I felt like going up to him to tell him: 'Don't shake the tassels of your Turkish topi so hard, my friend. This way you reveal yourself to be a Hindu. Arey, baba, this tassel is giving away your secret. Without it you don't appear Hindu. In the lines of your face, in the style of your dress, in the manner of your speech—neither is a Hindu visible, nor a Muslim.

'I know you. Only I. Will you allow me to offer you my salaam?'

1 November

I bear some hatred towards political parties. A swarm of the germs of spirituality live inside me. But I can see despite them that politics has entered through the doorway of life. And the steps of its dance, its song and its horrifying government have caused a turmoil inside me. The germs of spirituality and the healer of politics are constantly agitating each other. This is why the mind is often cloudy. There is no clarity.

I have been thinking about the Communist Party for two days. Only a few members live at the party office, where I am staying these days. But who knows what magic they carry because it seems as if these handful of people have the run of our entire universe. A war is raging outside. A calamity has fallen on lakhs of people. But these comrades have a strange quiet in their hearts, a pure and white peace. As if this terrible tragedy of history has not worried them in the least. As if they all know why this hell broke loose. I know some of it too. But in their knowing and my knowing there is definitely a big difference. Because I lack that whiteness of peace, those waves of satisfaction inside me. I wonder how this steadiness may be realized. Would I find this stability if I became a party member? But no, I am not a fan of miracles. It is much better to remain numb than to be living in the hope for miracles, and to be relieved of this crisis and pain of thought and worry.

I experience a strange kind of gentle pleasure and joy in walking around the different rooms of the Party Office, although there is no shortage of such buildings and rooms in Lahore. But in these ordinary rooms with their walls made of brick and cement, and the windows in them, they have an extraordinary unknown substance mixed inside. Or else why would

I experience this heavenly sensation of joy? What could this substance be? Would I find it? Would it be a solid, material substance? Or fine and delicate? There's a fragrance that runs through the rooms and the courtyard and perfumes the walls, and some rays escape these rooms that perfume the evenings of my life.

These are not even some strange or weird rooms. Those who sit in these rooms are not any different in bodily ways. Still, it feels as if they were meant to sit, speak and walk these rooms. If you remove them or displace them in the slightest from here, then the very structures of the attractions of these rooms will come falling down.

These people are the right examples of this machine age. Each of these comrades has become a machine. 'Hello, hello!' Mansoor is speaking to someone on the phone. 'Yes, yes. Two of our comrade doctors are performing their duties at the Wagah Camp. They are providing first aid to the refugees arriving from eastern Punjab—Hello, hello!—What did you say? The injections have run out? Okay, okay. I will try to arrange them now.'

The phone rings again.

'What? You are speaking from D.A.V. Camp?'*—

---

*The D.A.V. College in Lahore served as a refugee camp in 1947. Now, Islamia College occupies the erstwhile premises of D.A.V College Lahore, which moved to Ambala in India after Partition.

Five of our comrades are serving there—alright. So your wife and child have been left behind in a house in Shah Alami?* I will send a comrade there right away.'

A group of four–five Muslim Jats has entered the Party Office with a Sikh family.** Comrade Aslam is welcoming them. The Muslim Jats are saying: 'My friend, we have saved this family by risking our lives. Can you please deliver them to the camp now?'

Fair and handsome youths have arrived from Kashmir. They have sat down to discuss the Kashmir issue. The attention of all comrades is now focused here. Those youths seem nervous, and are arguing in favour of tribal aggression. And comrades Shaukat, Aslam, Mansoor and Mirza are explaining in a lucid and firm manner that they should not turn Kashmir into a pawn of the imperialists. And both the Kashmiri youths are looking at the comrades with suspicion, and think them to be agents of the Indian government.

And all of this goes on daily. Every day is the same frenzy, the same excitement, the same sincere agitation. Just now a short comrade has walked in to report that he had rescued the goods of a refugee from a dangerous area and was bringing them on a horse

---

*One of the largest market areas of Lahore.

**Jat: a warrior-peasant caste of the north-Indian subcontinent, mainly belonging to the Punjab and modern Haryana, but also found in Uttar Pradesh, Rajasthan, Sindh.

cart, when some goons arrived and stole the cart away with the goods. He had barely managed to escape in time with his life.

Such things happen every day in front of my eyes. And I keep looking in great wonder at the stony comrades who live in this stony monument, and think how will this purity be born into my soul? Will becoming a Party member do it? Will I attain the light that is inside them?

Comrade Mansoor's eyes seemed to respond to me in silence: by joining the Party you will accomplish nothing, O Poet! Become a member of life and its struggles. Membership is not accepted here for the sake of fashion or extravagance. But that purity, that light is born naturally inside those who jump into the struggle for life, into the soul of those who touch its pulse, which you confuse with membership. Rise up, rise up. Go jump into the fray of this new life, into this new storm! This storm that will give life a decisive peace and happiness—to the end, the last and the lasting.

3 November

My desire to leave Lahore has gotten stronger again. But there is no obstinacy and petulance driving this desire now, nor is there any anxiety or escapism. In fact, a shining ray of light has come piercing all these emotions. Every day I see trucks full of Hindu and

Sikh refugees as I cross the Mall Road, and I feel as if they are all pulled towards the graveyard in the terrible shade of the night. I do not see a ray of life on anyone's face. These burnt-out, sad and depressed faces carrying a meagre vision of their futures in their hearts are piling into the trucks. I want to stop each of these trucks, and loudly ask these people to take me with them so that I can also watch them dragging their feet in their independent and prosperous country. So that my eyes can look upon that sight where your little children, wives, mothers, sisters and women shiver in the bitter cold to give up their lives at the doorstep of the goddess of freedom. I wish you knew that in the country of your religion you would have to deal with sodden and burnt farms, ruined houses and bloodied and fiery streets. The arms that will open for you will not harbour the cool breezes of heaven, springs of honey and the gurgling river of love and beauty. Because a few robbers control this embrace. And the robbers do not want you to be acquainted with the beautiful vision of a free life. You will be released like cattle into the dry and arid jungle of the camps. Instead of being able to shout and scream, and heading for a lush grazing field, you will have to cool the hell-fires of your stomach with dry and bitter grass. And you will be burnt in the flames of your own hell.

But the trucks are roaring ahead with great speed.

And my desire to leave Lahore is growing stronger. I want to go to the Indian union to see the end of these weary faces. To see them die their deaths. Or, if possible, to extend to them the offerings of my art with a new conception of life. To take a group of writers from the Indian Union and tour every village, town and city and camp. And tell them: 'Friends, these are the characters for your works of art. Are you looking at their condition? Look. Look at these stars of your hopes. And write for them. And tell them that we need delicate, great, beautiful and content characters for our art, our great literature. Not weak, sunburnt, meaningless, lifeless failures and hopeless characters. Not for you, but for ourselves, we wish to give birth to these beautiful and great characters inside you, with voices that carry power, accents that resonate, eyes that are fresh, alert and sparkle, and souls that have width and aspiration.

The Quaid-e-Azam had arrived in Lahore this evening. It had been four months since the unfortunate Punjab got independence and had been wallowing in blood and dirt, and our beloved leader had remembered us only now. Maybe, the news of our destruction reached him late, and he had run forward in desperation to meet us. So, now, wave upon wave of a devastated and sad horde of people was heading forth to hear him. Everyone was trying to anticipate in their heart—what would our Quaid-e-Azam pronounce now? Will there be any comprehensive solution to our difficulties and failures? This is why legion upon legion of the world was breaking into the assembly ground. And a few friends and I had gathered to hear his speech on the radio. Firdausi Islam was reading his salutational poem. There was restlessness, excitement and a sense of expectation in the people. The announcer was commenting in his unique courtly manner on the ambience of the gathering. It felt as if everyone was waiting for the arrival of a king. I asked a comrade: 'Such kingly manners in these times of democracy? Why? But why?'

'We've gotten independence after three hundred years.* This is why we need to give the full evidence of our slavery,' that comrade replied. The Quaid-e-Azam was saying: 'Mujahids of the nation, you must be ready to offer more sacrifice.'** And the public had been startled into alertness. Will this continuum of sacrifices ever be broken? We want peace and rest. Why are we being asked for sacrifices again? We

---

*'Three hundred years' [of colonial rule]: This is factually incorrect, and a common error or misconception. Robert Clive won the Battle of Plassey in 1757, which is the first decisive British victory and counting from that date on, the British may be said to have ruled India for 190 years.

**Mujahid: One who does jehad or who strives against injustice and oppression, often held to be practiced by unbelievers in Islam, kaffirs, or non-Muslims.

risked our lives for independence. Now we wish for pleasure and happiness in our lives—such thoughts were passing through the minds of the gathering, but could not come to their lips.

After speaking for four–five minutes, the Quaid-e-Azam declared: 'Hereon, my speech will be in English, because the international press representatives do not understand our tongue.' And all our comrades were thinking, 'Is this speech for foreign representatives? Or to console and comfort the demoralized and devastated people?'—and the crowd was listening to the English speech like mute, deaf and blind people. As if asking, What is your command for us, O Quaid? Come sit with us and speak to us in our tongue. Remain our beloved…

But the speech continued. 'Cheers' were given. Because the rise and fall of the leader's words had a dramatic song-like lilt. It was attractive and full of belief. And the faithful public gathered, despite not understanding anything, understood that the words came from the mouth of their Quaid, therefore they must hold the panacea to all our griefs.

6 November

Yesterday again I stayed with Rahi in a plush mansion. This building is not his own, but neither has it been occupied by anyone else. Hence, the building is in the trust of Rahi and Hameed. Melody and feelings reside in Hameed's throat.* He went on smoking bidis the whole night, and singing the rich and flavourful songs of Saigal and Shamshad to us. And we kept trying to flow with the sweetness and intoxication of his songs. But even the songs of Saigal and Shamshad did not seem to have the capacity to absorb us away from our dissatisfaction, even if we kept superficially swaying and humming along with Hameed as he sang.

'My chunni is like a wave.'**

I was asking Rahi: 'Rahi, explain just this one point to me. It is the one confusion in my mind. This exquisitely painful line, "My chunni is like a wave", comes from which culture? Is it inscribed as the cultural legacy of Islam? Has Hindu culture given birth to it? After all, don't all our hearts leap in joy upon hearing it? Which is that harp in the depths of our souls that this line strums? And why? Our whole body reverberates with it. Why don't I find this reverberation in the Qur'an? Why don't I see it in the Vedas and the Grantha? Does only western Punjab have the right over its resonance? Does only the heart of eastern Punjab reverberate with it?

---

*The author uses rasa from the Sanskritik rasa in the original, which is quite untranslatable into English and has a whole aesthetic theory behind it in Sanskrit poetics. Here it is translated into one of its meanings as 'feelings'.

**'*Meri chunni ler ki taraan*'—the original is a line from a Punjabi folk song.

These two pieces? Will we divide this echo into two as well?

There was a lump in Rahi's throat then. He had seen the wound naked. But—his still lips seemed to be quietly saying—Comrade Fikr! This chunni has indeed become just like a wave now. The Punjab itself is a chunni—beautiful, colourful, undulating. But it has now been shredded. Could we join the scraps ever again? And this chunni? Will it wave in the land of the five rivers to the same melody and tune? Hameed, my friend. Sing another song. Anything else. A bad ghazal. Any pedestrian tappa.* Any common song in which I cannot see this Punjab with its chunni. Where the dirges of the murder of its verdant farms and swaying crops are not heard. Where the flowing blood of the pious and radiant honours of its daughters, girls, mothers and sisters may not be visible.

But Hameed had grown quiet. His stock of bidis was over. And he had no money either, with which he could have bought more to keep the river of his songs flowing. The youthful and rising singer-composer. An important pillar of the living culture of the country, a keeper of the secrets of people's hearts. This artist? He could have continued his song with bidis worth two paisas. But money? Where had money gone? Where had bidis run away? And he said to his brother, who

---

*Tappa: Punjabi folk song, often sung at weddings and full of romantic mischief or bawdy lyrics.

was a painter, and had escaped with his life from Amritsar, and had been looking everywhere in the heat and dust for work for one and a half months: 'Go tomorrow and ask that vile publisher to pay up the compensation for your pictures. Or stop giving him your work.'

Thereafter, Rahi began telling me his Amritsar stories. At the very mention of Amritsar his eyes would grow moist. He remembered the names of every street, each locality, all hotels, and every park of Amritsar and their exact locations to an astounding level. Amritsar is his birthplace. The city ran through his veins. He had lived the most beautiful and the most bitter moments of his life in its streets. He would adopt a highly tearful manner while speaking. And despite his highly emotional way, he could not bring himself to ask me: Fikr bhai, would I ever be able to go back to Amritsar? Will I ever walk around its streets and bazaars with complete abandon as my own? Maybe not, maybe not!—as if his eyes were replying without ever having posed the question.

Perhaps, yes, perhaps, yes! I wished to say to him: Rahi, Amritsar's streets are waiting for you. Your footprints are inscribed on them. You had sung the songs of freedom in the workers' movement there with thousands of starving and unfortunate humans. Those thousands of workers and peasants are waiting for you. They will never forget you. They await you. They have been conned terribly in the name of freedom. Comrade Rahi, the flagbearers of your vision, the translators of your views, the trustees of your heartbeat and the characters of your songs are still tossing about in hunger and thirst. The springs of your songs will once again flow through the factories of Amritsar, its mills and farms. Get up, you get up again. What happened? If today your starving workers' and peasants' wrinkles of toil have been covered by sprinkling the glorious colours of religious exploitation over them, they cannot remain hidden forever. Those stains, that kings and prophets have made, cannot be wiped out. And these kings and prophets are starting to lose their wits upon seeing the workers rise and come towards them with eyes full of wrath.

Rahi's eyes were glued to the ceiling. Maybe he wanted to tear it open to escape outside, but he had found no way through. Instead, he had to make way, for his art, for his views, for his peasants, the workers, for the starving and the naked.

He went on gazing at the ceiling.

7 November

A short soldier stopped me: 'Hey, hey, where are you going? Who are you?'

Chaudhari, Arif, Rahi, and Sahir looked at me with a smile. A tearful melody rose inside me: 'Life has come to a divide.'

The Gurkha soldier of D.A.V. camp, who was the protector of Hinduism, Hindu culture, Hindu rule and Hindu atmosphere, was asking me: 'Who are you? This is a Hindu camp. Are you Hindu? If you are Hindu then what have you been doing in Lahore for so long? You should have come to this camp on 15 August. You should have…'

I bared my forearm to the Gurkha soldier, showing the blue Om tattoo I have had since my childhood. The Gurkha soldier had got the proof of my Hinduism. He had approved my entry into the camp. And Sahir, Arif, Chaudhari, Jabir and Rahi were left on the other side of the line of Hinduism and Hindutva. Those five Muslims could not step on my land. For the first time in my life, I felt intense hatred towards Hindu religion. Prior to this, I had never considered such a casual thing as religion worth the hallowed and grand sentiment of my hatred.

I became restive. For a moment it felt as if my heart were struck by a bolt of lightning and that I should not enter this camp at all. All five of my Muslim friends were looking at me from afar with their arms extended wide open. Oh! Sahir, Arif, Rahi, Chaudhari, Jabir! Stay! I am coming now! I won't let such muddled things as this Gurkha soldier, this Hindutva line and this Hindu camp enter my life. I am coming to you. I am not going anywhere. Stop, stop. I won't go!

And abruptly throwing my luggage aside I crossed

the line drawn by the Gurkha soldier and came to the other side, where Sahir stood with his arms spread wide and said: 'Comrade Fikr! I apologize on behalf of all of Islam, for you could not live here.' And this statement of Sahir's descended echoing into the depths of my soul. The corners of Chaudhari's lips were again curling up in a way as if they were getting ready to laugh out in guffaws. But Chaudhari could not break into his guffaws. Go on Chaudhari, laugh! Do not keep this guffaw inside. Earlier, the feeling of good-health and strength was found in your guffaws. Now the guffaw that is forming upon your lips is sarcasm—at this melancholy and helplessness that prevails on this camp. Arif can neither laugh nor cry. He looks weary from excessive dejection, as if all of this is being constructed on the corpse of his hopes and dreams. All of those five Muslims—they kept sitting by my side for an hour. And kept trying to alleviate my sense of loss and pangs of separation. And the Gurkha soldier and other Hindus of the camp kept staring at us. They were rubbing their eyes and wondering how this newly admitted Hindu had developed such trust with these Muslims. A Muslim can never be sincere and truthful. He is a poisonous snake that bites on the sly. This Hindu must be a *fifth columnist* who is speaking to the Muslims in this friendly manner.*

---

*Fifth Columnist appears in English in the original.

And then the Gurkha soldier's crisp and stern voice was heard: 'Oi, you! You come here. You can't talk for this long.' All the five malechhas embraced me before going away, and I came with my head bowed and joined the sheep of my religion. The Gurkha soldier was looking at me with suspicion, in keeping with his character.

And then—and then it were as if I had spun around the whole universe as I sat dumbstruck and mute for half an hour. A storm was creating an uproar all around me—the racket of big, scary trucks, the hubbub of Hindu and Sikh refugees. A crowd of refugees had gathered outside the office of the camp commander that wanted roti, wanted wood to burn. It was demanding for the return of its abducted daughters, its plundered belongings. And the guns and bayonets of the soldiers guarding the commander were preventing the crowd from entering. I got up and half-heartedly toured the camp from one end to the other. An unending restlessness. A ceaseless discomfort. Refugees were coming and going. Some were shouting. Some were wailing loudly. A piece of someone's heart had been burnt away in a fire.* Someone's daughter-in-law had been stripped and raped in front of their eyes. An old woman was shrieking with loud howls: 'I don't want to go! I don't

---

*Piece of heart: Usually idiomatic for a parent's child.

want to go to your India! Bring me my little one! My babe! I give a damn for your freedom, for your India, without him. I don't want a free country! I want my baby!' A middle-aged woman going by tried to comfort the old woman: 'Ma! You at least have tears, I too want to cry for my only two-year-old, but these cursed eyes have no tears anymore!'

Four soldiers were coming in carrying two corpses on a stretcher, and were loading them on a truck to take them for their cremation. The truck which belonged to the Muslim military carried the two bodies away. It came to light that these two had perished last night due to hunger and weakness. A countrywoman was crying inconsolably as she held on to the coat of the lady doctor of the camp, and was getting dragged along behind her. She had a wrapped bundle under her arm. 'In the name of dharma, in the name of Lord Rama and Krishna, please save my child!' And the lady doctor was saying: 'Stupid and ignorant woman. Hasn't left my coat since yesterday. Her child is dead. But she hasn't removed it from her embrace.'

A storm of filth, rot and stink had arisen around the camp. Thousands of men, women and children were finding nourishment in this rot. Here and there, filth was piled up in stacks. One couldn't breathe in the stink. But despite these showers of filth and stink there were people who were still walking around imagining the independent and beautiful India to come. Everyone held on to the same hope in their heart that tomorrow they will reach the country of their dharma.

But to reach the country of their dharma they needed trucks. And trucks were to be gotten through referrals, recommendations and intercessions. And these were to be gotten through money. And money had disappeared. And people were distressed. But the camp's responsible caretakers believed that the people's distress was completely meaningless and a false allegation. These people are always clamouring for more and never understand the difficulties that the government faces.

An old man with a stick—not caring a jot for the government's difficulties, but having received a few pushes and shoves for it—came out of the crowd. He told me that he had been pushed around this way for a full two months already, and was surviving on the dry, old rotis of the camp. But he couldn't find a place on an India-bound truck. The rot and stink of the camp had caused two young ones in his family to be swallowed by death. And if they spent two-three more months here, they would all meet the same fate. I couldn't help but smile wryly, and my smile was asking, if this rot is nothing but the result of the festering and decay of the corpse of dharma?

A robust young soldier from the frontier region was fighting with a barber. A crowd had gathered because of the fight. And they were all cursing this

Pathan-looking soldier. The frontier soldier was telling the barber: 'Make the middle section of my moustache triangular. Because for many generations, this has been our way.' But it was the view of the barber and the gathered dhoti-clad Hindu crowd that this was a Muslim tradition, and now as they go forth into their Hindu country they should eschew this malechha tradition. This is a sin, forbidden in Hindu dharma. The shastras do not allow for such a moustache at all! But this philosophy of the shastras, sin and dharma was not registering in the head of the frontier soldier. He was bent on getting his moustache shaped into a triangle. Are all of these people really stupid? Such stupidity was at least never seen in Peshawar. We have had this tradition for so many generations. Then how can this be dharma-destroying?

I smiled wryly again. This manner of smiling was entirely new and completely fresh. Today, composite culture was being ripped apart into little shreds, and the overlords of religion with their fiery eyes wanted to wipe everything which had been the product of centuries of civilization. Today, the frontier's youth's religion was getting reinvigorated. And an unsuccessful attempt was being made to give life to the dead and bowed skeletons of the shastras and puranas. It seemed that the meanings of emotions, traditions, demands and claims had changed immediately upon winning independence. Why had such freedom been brought into existence? Was it only to free dharma and shastras that we had struggled for three hundred years against foreign rule? Did we strive to move forward or only to go back by thousands of years? Did we call to freedom only for life to regress?

Prolonged and recurrent smiles full of venom had wearied my whole body. Tired, I came and sat upon the bench near the Gurkha soldier. Seeing me dismayed and sad, the Gurkha soldier came and sat next to me. 'You get very, very sad. What is the matter? What used to be your job?' I said without raising my head: 'I am a poet, I write poems.' The Gurkha soldier almost jumped up: 'Poems! You are such a good man. For whom do you write these poems?' I was a little startled, 'For you. For these starving and naked people. For those refugees.'

'Then recite a poem to a refugee. This refugee is very sad, cries a lot. Muslims kill them. Loot them. Burn their homes. Recite your poems to him. Give him relief!' My interest increased. I took hold of his gun and said: 'But you know who gets this refugee killed? Who sets the fires? Who makes them fight?'

'I know everything. I know everything. But what can I say? I am a servant of the state. If I open my mouth, I will be immediately fired.'

And the extinguished spark of my soul was rekindled again. It felt as if my chest had shone and illuminated the whole camp. And the uncouth group of destitute and desperate humans had transformed into a company of Gurkha soldiers. All their dim and lifeless eyes were saying: 'We know everything, we know everything, but if we spoke out, then…then… then…'

Chaudhari had come back. He was calling to me from outside the big gate of the camp. He had come with a basket of flowers in his hands, and with Mufti by his side. I ran to them. Mumtaz ran up and pulled me into an embrace. He had got a lump in his throat. The waves of happiness boiling out of Chaudhari's veins reached his lips and came out as his joyful guffaw. He had brought Mufti along for us to meet. And with his joyful guffaws was putting an end to our bitter differences.

Mufti had brought a pack of cigarettes for me. And we both smoked them, and ate fruits for a while. And the Gurkha soldier kept smiling at us, looking on with meaningful eyes from distance. As if saying: 'But what can I do? I am a state servant. If I speak a word, then…'

On their way out, Chaudhari took out the pen from Mufti's pocket and kept it in mine, saying: 'Keep this as his remembrance.' And he laughed out his joyful guffaw again in warning to me.

8 November

Today I sit as a refugee in the Khalsa College Camp of Amritsar.* There is a mass of women, children, the old and the young spreading all around me for two to two-and-a-half miles. There are trucks and tents. The city is not new to me. But for this crowd it is a new country, a new nation. They have breathed a sigh of contentment upon arrival.

This is why Diwali is being celebrated in Khalsa camp today. Electric lights have been lit to brighten and illuminate the place. There is music, accompanied with speeches and sermons of peace. But the people have created a tumult. They cannot sit quietly in the assembly. There is no peace or quiet in their hearts. Their homes have been destroyed. Their beloved neighbours have been turned into enemies and taken from them. Their crops lie waste. Their children have bitten the dust and rolled in blood. Humanity is ashamed at the acts perpetrated on their young daughters. The heads of their wives, mothers and old fathers have been removed from their bodies. The novel of their life has been taken to its climax and then turned tragic. And they are restless and agitated. This sermon of peace does not go down their throats. The

---

*Fikr found out only upon reaching Amritsar, from his cousin whom he couldn't first recognize as they had been separated in childhood, that his wife and daughter had reached Ambala camp.

gloom of their heart cannot be removed by the lamps of Diwali. A huge sea of darkness billows inside and around them.

And a Diwali celebration is on at Khalsa College Camp. As if Lord Rama, having vanquished the wicked Ravana, is entering Ayodhya, in victory and glory. He is being welcomed by light, lustre, beauty and ornaments. A nationalist present in the assembly was saying: 'Today we have clearly defeated the English. Come let us celebrate our first Diwali in style.' The crowd shouted back: 'Give us our rations. Give us wood. Give us vegetables. Give us milk. Give us clothes. We are hungry. We will not celebrate Diwali! Put out the lamps. Turn off the lights. Come and scream and shout as loudly as you can. Cry, let your tears flow. So that with the warmth of your tears all these speeches, this music and these songs may melt away!'

And I was remembering how these very people were so eager to get away from Lahore's D.A.V. College camp to India. With what enthusiasm and hope they had loaded their baggage on the trucks. How they had then loaded themselves like goats and sheep on the trucks! How the soldiers had chided, threatened and abused them! They had pushed and shoved them. But they were so firm in their faith that despite all these humiliations and insults they had still wished to come to India.

The Muslim military was to accompany the trucks as their protectors. This is why the hearts of all the sheep loaded on the trucks were palpitating with fear. Their throats remained dry until the journey came to an end. Their lips gathered scum. Their breath had been stifled inside. But they had remained silent. And had gone on shivering, remained timid and scared. What trust on the Muslim military? The trucks had to be halted many times on the way, for different legal and organizational reasons. And every time the crowds atop them had thought that this was it, they were done for now. The Muslim military will stand them in a line and, bang, shoot them dead. The 13-mile road between Lahore and Amritsar was traversed in three hours. And when these trucks had reached the border, then on one side of them, the tricolour was flying with great pride and respect. Upon seeing the tricolour the mouths of all the sheep opened and they started bleating. Sleepy lips woke up. Dim eyes got a spark, numb hands and feet started moving, and all of them shouted together:

'Long live Hindustan!'

'Long live Pandit Jawaharlal Nehru!'

'Now we have reached our country. No one can harm us here.'

'Long live revolution!'

Slogans were being shouted every two minutes. How hollow was this happiness, this joy? There were undercurrents of fear, envy, hatred and enmity behind it. My throat had gone dry. I couldn't cry out even the feeblest of slogans. The people sitting on my truck had looked at me with hateful eyes, and I had started looking in the opposite direction of the truck. Under the flag, a board read, 'The Government of Pakistan'.

And a caravan of trucks carrying Muslim refugees had come from India and stopped at the border. And they were shouting slogans:

'Long live Pakistan!'

'Long live Quaid-e-Azam!'

A crowd had gathered next to one truck of this caravan. A few military soldiers were lowering the body of a middle-aged man. It came to be known that because of excessive weakness his arms had jammed while holding on to the rod of the truck, and in extreme hunger and thirst he had fallen off the moving truck to his death. Death was adopting such bizarre and uncanny ways. There was no longer a standard or a trial required to die. Go stiff standing on a truck and die. Die of the stink of camps. Die of floods. Die at seeing your young daughter being taken by the goons. Die at seeing your child hanging from the ceiling. And then shout out the slogans:

Long live India!

Long live Pakistan!

Long live Jawaharlal Nehru!

Long live Quaid-e-Azam!

And then, from the border of Wagah to Amritsar our trucks continued to resound with such slogans. These slogans had turned into a large and continued stampede and bewilderment by the time we reached Khalsa camp. The camp was glittering with the light of lamps. But our hearts still carried a wretched darkness. Freedom's sweet and enthusiastic vision was being shattered. Where will we go now? What will we do now? In this independent nation, who will give us a place to sleep, bread to fill our stomachs and cloth to cover our bodies? Who is he? Who is that person? Who told us that you are free now and are free to play romantic games with the moon and the stars? That their stellar assembly will gather? That the dawn's gleaming and invigorating splendour will rise up in your souls? Billows of the soft and sweet morning breeze will bring a beautiful and magical future to your life?

Where is that future?

Where is the dawn?

Where is azadi?

Come, friends. We have been served an incredible lie. A dangerous gambit has been played against us. Our search and quest and struggle have all been frozen. Come, come, this is not that dawn, nor that destination, for which we had striven. Come, let us go further. Further, still further, and still further ahead. Today, new fogs, new darkness, and new obscurities have been erected around us. Come, let us pierce through them. Let us vault over them. And try to look for the footsteps of that dawn whose impressions have swayed in the hidden depths of our hearts for three hundred years.

The crowd was shouting slogans as per tradition:
'We will not celebrate Diwali!'
'Give us roti!'
'Give us clothes.'
'Give us homes.'
'We will not celebrate Diwali!'

Appendix I: The Fikr Bibliography

Urdu (Nastaliq)

1. *Hayule* (1947)
2. *Chhata Darya* (1948)
3. *Mao Zedong* (1954)
4. *Professor Buddhu* (1961)
5. *Pyaz ke Chhilke* (1965)
6. *Warrant Giraftari* (1966)
7. *Chaupat Raja* (1973)
8. *Fikriyaat* (1974)
9. *Badnaam Kitab* (1975)
10. *Fikr Nama* (1977)
11. *Aadha Aadmi* (1980)
12. *Baat Mein Ghaat* (1983)
13. *Ghar Mein Chor* (1983)
14. *Chhilke hi Chhilke* (1984)
15. *Fikr Bani* (1986)
16. *Pyaz ke Chhilke, Part II* (1986)
17. *Main* (1987)
18. *Meri Biwi* (1987)
19. *Modern Alladin* (1987)

20. *Akhri Kitab* (1987)
21. *Satvan Shastra* (1987)
22. *Chand Aur Gadha* (1987)
23. *Teer-e-Neemkash* (1987)
24. *Khado Khel* (1987)
25. *Kafan se Kurte Tak* (1988)

Hindi (Nagari)

1. *Hum Hindustani*
2. *Swatantrata ke Baad Ka Sarwashrestha Urdu Haasya Vyang* (Edited)
3. *Badnaam Kitaab* (1977)
4. *Raja Raj Kare* (1974)
5. *Darling*
6. *Warrant Giraftari*
7. *Modern Alladin*
8. *Gumshuda ki Talaash*

Translator's Acknowledgements

First thanks are due to Mr Phool Kumar Bhatia, the son of Fikr Taunsvi, who gave me the rights to translate *Chhata Darya*. Secondly, but first in the chronological order of events, I must express my gratitude to Dr Rakhshanda Jalil for pointing me towards Fikr, and publishing excerpts of *The Sixth River* in her co-edited volume, *Looking Back* (Orient Blackswan, 2017). Kanishka Gupta pushed me to complete the translation of the full journal, send out book proposals, and connected me with Ravi Singh, who showed great interest in Fikr. Charles Wallace India Trust funded a three-month Writing and Translation fellowship at Aberystwyth, Wales, based at the Mercator Institute and with Literature Across Frontiers with Prof. Elin Jones and Alexandra Buchler, where I undertook the bulk of the translation. My mother, Akhtari Begum, has always been my pillar of support and helps me quite frequently with the nuances of Urdu. I cannot thank her enough. Conversations with Lipika Kamra and Uttaran Das

Gupta succoured me through this period, and they read through drafts and gave comments. Dr Shahena Tabassum helped me avail the *Biswi Sadi* issue on Fikr Taunsvi. Dr Albeena Shakil suggested some useful directions for the Introduction. My warm gratitude to both. All the blurb givers, Prof. Ayesha Jalal, Ms Urvashi Butalia, Prof. Ayesha Kidwai, Dr Tarun Saint and Dr Pippa Virdee, were immensely kind, as they gave wonderful commendations based on the merits of the work, with little or no prior acquaintance with me. Tarun also gave close comments on the text. Radhika Shenoy proved to be an excellent copyeditor. Mrs Rani Ahuja, daughter of Fikr, responded with great enthusiasm to my translation and gave useful feedback. Finally, Fikr Taunsvi deserves all the accolades for this searing testimony on partition, and I hope the English translation does it justice and carries it further.

ALSO FROM SPEAKING TIGER

THE UNSAFE ASYLUM
Stories of Partition and Madness
Anirudh Kala

After Partition, India exchanged the Muslim patients in its Mental Hospitals for their Hindu and Sikh counterparts in Pakistan. These interlinked short stories explore the impact of this decision, together with the ongoing consequences of Partition. Rulda Singh and Fattu (Fateh Khan), patients at Lahore's Mental Hospital, are separated, possibly for ever. Years later, Prakash Kohli, an Indian psychiatry student, hears Rulda's account of his journey to India, with its casual official cruelty and unexpected tenderness. When he visits Lahore, Prakash discovers the story of his own birth in 1947, forms a lifelong friendship with a Pakistani colleague—and realizes that nobody knows why so few mental patients survived the exchange.

As Prakash becomes curious about this, he realizes that Partition continues to have a profound effect on the psyches of his patients. A middle-aged woman passes on a delusion of being chased by murderous mobs to her children. A young boy from Simla is convinced that Benazir Bhutto, the Pakistani President's daughter, loves him and they have discussions in his dreams every night. And Prakash, seeing Punjab go up in flames under a militant call for another land of the pure, wonders if Partitions can happen again.

These stories, and more, with their recurring and shared characters, remind us that Partition does not merely lie in the past. Powerful and unsettling, this collection is essential reading.

ALSO FROM SPEAKING TIGER

WEAVING WATER
An Autobiography

Ajeet Cour

*Translated from the Punjabi by
Masooma Ali and Meenu Minocha*

Heartwarming and candid, this is the story of one of our foremost literary voices, told in her own words—a life beset by tragedy which yet carries a message of couragebh, hope and happiness.

Growing up in pre-Partition Lahore, Ajeet Cour spent a childhood wrapped in warm and enticing experiences, despite her disciplinarian father. From such a beginning, her life moves on to a first, true love that is lost on account of a misunderstanding; a violent, bitter marriage that leaves her with two young children to support; the death of a beloved child, and the loss, again, of love when at last she seems to have found it. But despite the tragedy that always seems to follow her, Ajeet Cour's story is one of courage, hope and a sort of happiness, as she finds her eventual refuge in herself.

ALSO FROM SPEAKING TIGER

PRISON DAYS

Vijaya Lakshmi Pandit

Foreword by Nayantara Sahgal

'The author of this absorbing book was, where India is concerned, truly present at the Creation...I urge her book on everyone who lived in those great years and on all those who want to know more about them.'

—John Kenneth Galbraith

When Mahatma Gandhi gave the call for the nation to join in the freedom struggle, Vijaya Lakshmi Pandit threw herself wholeheartedly into the Movement, along with her father, Motilal Nehru, brother Jawaharlal, and husband, Ranjit Sitaram Pandit. *Prison Days* is an account of her third and final term in Naini Central Jail in Allahabad. She was arrested on 12 August 1942. World War II was on, the country was under military rule and arrest and imprisonment took place without trial. Several lorries filled with armed policemen arrived that night at Anand Bhawan to arrest one lone, unarmed woman.

Though it is more the personal, day-to-day details of her life that fill Pandit's jail diary, it is the politics of the day—the overarching desire to throw off the shackles of British rule and Mahatma Gandhi's unique approach of non-violence and non-cooperation to achieve this, that define the book. It is this that gives Vijaya Lakshmi Pandit and her fellow prisoners the courage to carry on the fight with unbroken spirits—and at the stroke of the midnight hour on 15 August 1947, victory was theirs. India was reborn as an independent nation.

www.ingramcontent.com/pod-product-compliance
Lightning Source LLC
Chambersburg PA
CBHW061941220426
43662CB00012B/1984